Front and back cover:
Taj Mahal
Pages 2/3:
Cambodia: Angkor, Bayon temple
Pages 6/ 7:
Sicily: Segesta
Page 11:
Cambodia: Angkor Thom
Page 112:
Moscow

Photographic credits:

Nguyen Thuc Diem: 1, 11, 34/35, 38/39, 46, 47, 48, 49, 51, 52/53, 54/55, 56, 57, 59, 62/63, 70/71, 73, 76, 84, 85, 86/87, 90/91, 92/93, 110, 112, 121, 122/123. **Hervé Champollion**: 6/7, 20/21. **Gros de Beler**: 22, 23, 40, 41, 44, 45, 98, 99, 100/101, 103, 106/107. **Eparzier:** 18/19. **Alain Mahuzier**: 26, 27, 89, 94, 95. **Slide/Bavaria**: 14/15, 16/17, 20/21, 29, 78/79. **Slide/Cash**: 12/13, 24, 25, 62/63, 70/71.**Slide/Viewfinder**: 38/39, 43 bas. **Slide/Visuals**: 80,108/109, 110/111. **Slide/Charmet**: 129. **Slide/Féjoz**: 36/37. **Slide/Kanus**: 104/105. **Slide/Petri**: 68/69, 82/83, 96/97. **Hirou/Yargui**: 98/99.

Contribution: F.B. S.B.

Published by Grange Books
an imprint of Grange Books Plc
The Grange
Kingsnorth Industrial Estate
Hoo, nr Rochester
Kent ME3 9ND
www.Grangebooks.co.uk
ISBN: 1-840136-88X

WONDERS
OF THE
WORLD

Foreword
Alain Mahuzier

Grange
BOOKS

FOREWORD

"My second home," my father used to say, "is the whole world." And with these words he took his wife and nine children with him on a world tour that began for me the day I was born.

And so I spent my life exploring the world and discovering all its infinite beauty. You too can admire the wonders of the world in this remarkable book, whose stunning photographs illustrate the marvels to be seen on five continents. Of the "Seven Wonders of the World" of antiquity only the awesome Pyramid of Cheops has survived, but our distant ancestors had built fabulous cities whose very names set us daydreaming: Persepolis, the treasure of the Persians, burnt to the ground by Thais, lover of Alexander the Great; and Baalbek in Lebanon, whose columns, rising against the desert sunset, fill you with such sweet melancholy.

Cities like Athens were world focal points for thought; like Jerusalem, shrines for all the monotheistic religions. Then there were temples like Angkor, centers of world art, and pyramids like Chichen Itza or Tikal, traces of vanished peoples.

But what of the mystery you sense in places that are much harder to visit, where unknown architectures arise abruptly out of the country-side: the temple of Apollo at Bassae, in Greece; the ancient city of Apollonia, in Albania; the ruins of Gondar in Ethiopia; and the famous Machu Picchu, last refuge of the Incas?

Who can fail to be amazed by the menhir-statues of San Agustin, or the treasure of Tutankhamen, the young pharaoh whose smile has been captured in gold for all eternity?

Yet the most awe-inspiring single place in the world is the most isolated: Easter Island. As we contemplate the moais, those enigmatic statues with their "eyes that look to the sky", an overwhelming sense of the cosmic brings home to us the closeness between the infinite extent of the universe and the infinite smallness of our planet.

The East is an inexhaustible source of wonders: the caravan cities of central Asia, with their reminders of Marco Polo and the Silk Routes; the temples of India, whose artists worked with such skill, and of Burma and Thailand. With their endless riches these "domains of the gods" extend to the furthest reaches of Japan, sometimes seeming the work of giants, sometimes creating a delicate balance between stone, gold and earth. In Tibet you will experience the strangeness of a Buddhist art that seems to echo an earlier world, fragments of which live on in your subconscious.

Yet among the "wonders of the world" are also the splendors of nature. One is dumbstruck by the colossal grandeur of Bryce Canyon in the pink-tinged sunset, by the extraordinary waterfalls of Angola and the spellbinding power of the Australian desert.

Modern man, too, has achieved extraordinary feats, such as the forests of skyscrapers of New York and Singapore. But perhaps Europe is home to the greatest beauties of world architecture: the treasures of London, the Grand-Place in Brussels, the Alhambra in Grenada, the gilded roofs of Prague, the cathedrals of the Kremlin, the gleaming palaces of the Tsars, or Topkapi, residence of the Ottoman sultans.

Think of the nostalgia that sweeps through us in Venice in the autumn; of the grandeur of the Château de Chambord in the Loire Valley; of King Ludwig's folly at Neuschwanstein. You will find them all in this book, an irresistible summons to dream, to travel, to get away from it all: wonders of the world no traveler can ever tire of.

Alain MAHUZIER
Filmmaker, lecturer

CONTENTS

Great Britain

London is the capital of England, but England is only part of the United Kingdom, which comprises Great Britain and Northern Ireland. Great Britain, as the sociologist André Siegfried emphasized, is "an island surrounded by water – and has been Anglican ever since the Pope forbade King Henry VIII to marry Ann Boleyn. Very much in love with the young woman, the colorful sovereign had no hesitation in breaking with Rome to wed her and at the same time proclaim himself spiritual leader of his people. Nor did he have any misgivings, some time later, about having his young bride executed and remarrying four times. Thus his private life was the deciding factor in the spiritual future of his subjects.

London's growth as a trading centre began with the Romans, who had established themselves there on an earlier Celtic site. Later there came the Vikings and the Barbarians. In the middle of the 11th century, Westminster – the "western", as opposed to the "eastern" monastery – was chosen as the heart of the kingdom. It was there that Edward the Confessor, king of England created the first seat of British power.

Between 1050 and 1065, Edward extended the monastery that was to become the first Palace of Westminster, but his cousin, William the Conqueror, seized the throne after his victory at Hastings in 1066. After his coronation at Westminster Abbey, William took up residence in the palace, which housed both the royal family and Parliament until the 106th century. Already, in the 14th century, the Parliament had been divided into the upper and lower houses: the House of Lords and the House of Commons. The Parliament was all but totally destroyed by fire in 1834, the only surviving parts being Westminster Hall, St Stephen's Crypt and the Jewel Tower. Among the spectators during the fire were Turner and Constable, who both produced paintings of the event. In 1840 Charles Barry and Augustus Pugin began rebuilding in the neo-Gothic style characteristic of the Victorian era. The House of Lords, with its handsome, engraved throne, was finished in 1847 and the House of Commons in 1850. After being destroyed by German bombing on 10 May 1941, the House of Commons was rebuilt and reopened in 1950.

London: Westminster

The political and religious upheavals of this country, whose influence spread to all five continents, often began within the walls of what was once a monastery on the banks of the Thames. Its size is mind-boggling: more than 1000 rooms, 100 staircases and 11 kilometers (7 miles) of corridors. There are two towers, the Clocktower and the Queen Victoria Tower. Finished in 1858, the Clocktower is 96 meters (over 300 feet high) and has become the symbol of the city of London. The clock itself weighs 13 tons. Nicknamed Big Ben – after Sir Benjamin Hall, who supervised its installation – it's sounding of the hours is used by the BBC. Parliament sits once a year: the British flag flies on the Queen Victoria Tower during day sessions, and the lantern atop the Clocktower lights up during night sessions.

Belgium

A region of Gaul, Belgium was part of the Roman Empire, then of the kingdom of the Franks. In the Middle Ages powerful fiefdoms were established there, among them the earldoms of Flanders and Brabant. The latter was absorbed by the House of Burgundy in 1406 and inherited by Duke Philip the Good in 1430. In 1477 Brabant was taken over by Austria. Situated in Brabant, Brussels grew up around a castle – known as bruoc sella, the house in the marsh – built in the late 10th century on one of the three islands in the river Senne.

From the 12th century onwards Brussels began to expand, developing its cloth industry and becoming a major trading centre and staging post between Cologne and Bruges. Trade prospered in the 13th and 14th centuries and the population increase brought changes to the look of the city. New ramparts went up between 1357 and 1379. In the early 15th century the dukes of Brabant decided to leave Louvain for Brussels. The city's aldermen asked the architect Jacques van Thienen to build the City Hall, and work began in 1402. Set on the Grand-Place, site of the city's market since the 12th century, the finished building is a masterpiece of Brabant's Flamboyant Gothic style. It is dominated by a splendid tower more than 90 meters (300 feet) high.

This busy spot is home to other historic monuments as well. The Maison du Roi ("The King's House"), now the city museum, dates from the 16th century. It was restored by Charles V, who was crowned in Brussels in 1516. Charles abdicated in 1,555in favor of his son Philip II, King of Spain like his father and sovereign of the Netherlands. The houses lining the square are famous as former meeting places for the city's trade corporations. After the bombardment by Louis XIV's troops in 1695 they were rebuilt in the Baroque style. Among the corporations represented were the Mercers, whose Maison du Renard ("House of the Fox") bears the statue of St Nicholas, their patron saint; the Archers (in the Maison de la Louve – "House of the She-wolf"); the Butchers ("By appointment to the King of Spain", as they were known); the Tailors, who met in the Chaloupe d'or (the "Golden Boat"); and the Painters (in the "House of the Pigeon"), where Victor Hugo lived in 1852.

Brussels: the Grand-Place

A reminder of the heyday of the corporations, this is one of the handsomest squares in all Europe. Its architectural style – a mingling of Gothic and Renaissance – is to be found in a number of other prosperous cities in northern Europe: the closed rectangle is surrounded by tall, narrow houses whose sculpted facades leave as much room as possible for the small-paned windows. To the left, the facade of the City Hall, sculpted as if it were a cathedral, points up the close relationship at the time between religious and civic life.

Germany

Of all the "mad hatter's castles" built by Ludwig II of Bavaria, Neuschwanstein is beyond doubt the most famous. Tall, slender and white, it is for many travelers the very emblem of Germany. Yet it does not always fit with our preconceived ideas of that country.

A little German history helps to clarify things. Only a hundred and thirty years ago Munich and Berlin were locked in bitter combat. Prussia, a largely Protestant, military-minded state, had a difficult relationship with Bavaria, mainly Catholic and on good terms with the Austro-Hungarian empire. In 1866 Bismarck's troops in their pointed helmets brutally crushed Austria in the Battle of Sadowa, together with Austria's ally Bavaria, which in 1871 was definitively incorporated into Germany.

Prussia had proved its superiority, but one of the strengths of the Holy Roman German Empire had always been its unity of language and culture; and as the last of the Wittelsbachs, an artistic dynasty determined to assert itself by peaceful, intellectual means, Ludwig had been raised on Germanic culture and the legends of the Nibelungen.

When his father died Ludwig was only 18: he at once assumed the throne and his first act was to send for the composer who had brought all these legends to the stage: Richard Wagner.

The relationship between Ludwig and Wagner generated all sorts of controversy: for the people of Bavaria Wagner was a foreigner and his whims were intolerable. Soon, with his political power taken from him by Bismarck, and Wagner far away, Ludwig returned to the Wittelsbach passion for the arts. His father, Ludwig I, had at one time wanted to rebuild Munich in the Gothic style as proof of the power of his capital city.

Despite an icy welcome from the French, for whom there was no difference between a Prussian and a Bavarian, the young sovereign was fascinated by Paris and Versailles on a visit to France. He returned the following year and a stay in Reims left him enthused by the divine legend of the Bourbons. These two visits to France left an indelible mark on Ludwig: Bavaria might have no political power, but like the Bourbons the Wittelsbachs were of divine lineage and, as he saw it, their native soil would be graced by his masterpieces.

Neuschwanstein Castle

Set at almost 1000 meters (3400 feet) above sea level, this extraordinary structure – its name translates as "the swan's new stone" – was Ludwig II's first venture into castle-building, but was still unfinished at his death in 1886. The first stone was laid on 5 September 1869, before Ludwig's visit to France. At the height of his Wagner period, and haunted by the tales of Siegfried, he had been thinking of a fortress on medieval lines; but then a stage designer presented him with a set of drawings he found irresistible. The second half of the 19th century saw an odd fashion for neo-Gothic in the West and here, the Romanesque, Rococo and Gothic merged with the young ruler's fantasies in a superbly surrealistic patchwork. Some of the rooms could serve without the slightest modification as theatres for Tannhaüser or Lohengrin. The sheer decorative profusion of the interior and the gigantic proportions – over 200 rooms were planned – gave rise to expenses that soon posed political problems for the king. It should be noted that this aesthete always chose superb sites for his castles, the three best known being Neuschwanstein, Herrenchiemsee (a replica of Versailles) and Linderhof, an Italianate version of the Petit Trianon, also at Versailles.

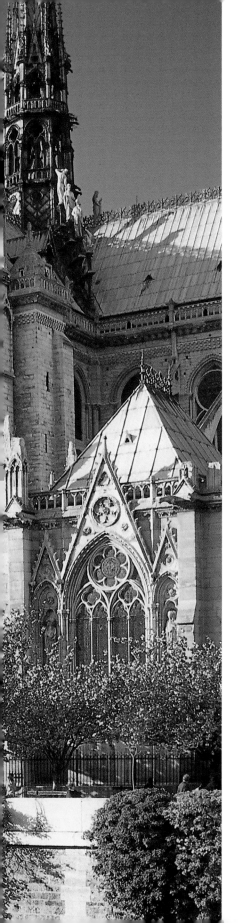

France: Paris

It seems that there was once a Celtic tribe, the Parisii, who settled on a stretch of marshland they saw as particularly fertile. This hospitable terrain would become an island; and when the Romans arrived they entrusted it to their talented architects. Once it became clear that the island was too small, a move into the area opposite – now the famous Left Bank – doubled the available space. This was increased further with the building of roads towards Rome and Spain, yet the original island remained the heart of Lutetia, as Paris was then called. It was home to the seat of government – built later, the prefect's palace is still used by the Prefect of Paris today; to the religious focal point, the temple of Jupiter – where Notre Dame now stands; and to the centre of public life – the Forum.

All too soon this era of prosperity was interrupted by the armies of Attila the Hun. The Lutetians from the Left Bank took refuge on the island, where St Genevieve urged them to fight – which they did, successfully.

Not long afterwards the Norsemen arrived from Scandinavia, sailing down the Seine and invading the territory of the Franks. Faced with repeated attacks, the people regrouped and chose a real leader: Odo (or "Eudes"), Count of Paris, became king. His successor put a stop to the Norse incursions by granting them Normandy. Then came Hugues Capet, elected Duke of Paris by his peers and proclaimed King of France in 987. Gradually the kingdom took shape. The Crusades attracted enormous public attention, with people coming to listen to clergymen who preached fiery sermons when not dispensing knowledge to voracious students: only the clergy were permitted to teach, whatever the subject. It was at this time that the brilliant cleric Abelard fell so unhappily in love with Heloise, niece of the famous Canon Fulbert. Already Abbé Suger had been the focus of all eyes with his superb rebuilding of the abbey at Saint-Denis, and when, in 1160, Maurice de Sully became Bishop of Paris, he obtained Louis VII's approval for the building of a cathedral worthy of a capital city. De Sully's vision of the future proved accurate: nine centuries later "his" cathedral, a true architectural jewel, was still one of the religious and artistic landmarks of the Western world.

Notre-Dame

The apse of the cathedral is often likened to the spread sails of a ship, in a further reference to the nautes, or river merchants, the first masters of the capital: their motto "Fluctuat nec mergitur" ("Shaken by the waves, but not sunk") is still part of the city's coat of arms. For all sorts of reasons Notre Dame, the heart of the island that was the cradle of Paris, retains enormous symbolic power. Although the capital is home to countless ancient churches and civic monuments, together with more recent constructions like the Eiffel Tower and the National Library, Notre Dame remains the city's emblem – and, curiously enough, a non-religious one.

19

Chambord

The Château de Chambord was François I's luminous gift to the France he so fervently wanted to reign over. At the dawn of the 16th century the country had only just emerged from that long period known as the Middle Ages, when the role of the King and his lords was to ensure food and physical safety for the people. France had a long tradition of being on the defensive: there had been the Viking invasions and the endless conflicts with England sparked by the marriage of Eleanor of Aquitaine to Henry II, King of England. Two centuries later the Hundred Years War (1337-1453) broke out. The end of the Middle Ages saw the English problem settled, but then came the wars with Italy, whose sumptuous cities and duchies would soon fascinate the whole of Europe.

In the very last years of the 15th century Charles VIII, son of Louis XI, provoked the outbreak of fresh hostilities by deciding to assert his mother's rights over the kingdom of Naples. In 1515 François of Angoulême, who had married the daughter of Louis XII a year earlier, carried off the legendary victory of the Battle of Marignan. Much impressed with the artistic richness he had seen in Italy, on his return to France he set about building the Château de Chambord. Very soon the site had given birth to a host of legends, one of them having to do with a hunting accident – a fall from a horse – that led Louis XII to be most tenderly cared for by the Countess de Thoury.

The identity of the architect has never been established with certainty: it may have been Domenico da Cortona, known as Boccador and designer of the Hôtel de Ville in Paris. Rumor also has it that a famous neighbor, Leonardo da Vinci, who lived at Clos-Lucé, made a contribution; but the only thing we can be really sure of is the Italian influence. With Chambord François I inaugurated a revolutionary new architectural concept: a castle designed solely for pleasurable living, with no fortifications whatsoever.

Despite its central keep, everything at Chambord reflects the new Renaissance fashions: windows with views stretching to the horizon, handsome terraces that were perfect for strolling. All in all, a luxury setting that was the complete opposite of what earlier castles had been.

Rear view of the château

Ten years after victory at Marignan, François I suffered disaster in the battle of Pavia and underwent the indignity of captivity. This made it extremely daring on his part to borrow the Italian enemy's artistic traditions for the building of a castle with no defenses at all. But like Xerxes at Persepolis and Pericles in Athens, France's "father of arts and letters" had understood the importance of ceremonial. When Charles V consented to visit Chambord at his invitation, it was clear that the gamble had paid off.

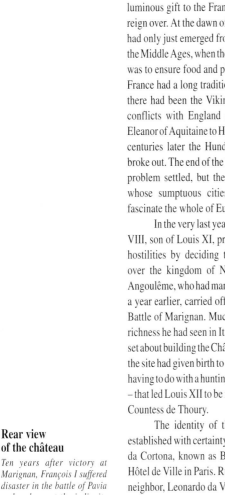

Spain

In 1492 the Catholic rulers Isabella of Castile and Ferdinand of Aragon, conquered Grenada (al-Garnati in Arabic), forcing Boabdil, the last Muslim king of Andalusia, to surrender. For two centuries the Nasrid Dynasty had benefited from the king's role as an intermediary for trade between the Christian kingdoms of Spain and the Muslim Maghreb, in North Africa. This period was the high point of Hispano-Moorish civilization.

The Calat Alhambra, or "red castle", is a royal fortress overlooking Grenada. To the west is the Alcazaba fortress, with its view over the vega, the broad plain sweeping all the way to the foot of the Sierra Nevada. To the east, the old city has been replaced by the El Partal gardens, while to the north is the Alcazar.

The Alhambra palace is built around two long patios running at right angles to each other. A handsome feature is the Comares Courtyard – also known as the Courtyard of Myrtles, because of the clumps of myrtle lining the long pool – with its arcades and ground level reception rooms: one of them, the Barca Room, was built under Yussuf I (1332-54). The Courtyard of the Lions, the Room of the Two Sisters (two enormous slabs of marble), the Stalactites Room, the Royal Courtroom and the Hall of the Abencerages – an aristocratic family executed by Boabdil – all date from the time of Mohamed V (1354-92). The Fountain of the Lions is set at the centre of two intersecting paths leading off to four pavilions.

Nasrid art in Grenada is an exercise in virtuosity, contrast and nuance: smooth walls set off by colonnades; changes of rhythm suggested by delicate little columns placed singly, in pairs and in groups; and rows of archways. The decoration is sumptuous: glazed earthenware mosaics with geometrical patterns, plasterwork sculpted with floral motifs and calligraphy, ceilings and domes of wood intricately sculpted or painted.

The Generalife, with its terraced gardens, was where the kings of Grenada came to relax. This is a land of cypress and laurel, of myrtle and orange trees, of pools and fountains. To the north and south are two pavilions with splendid porticos. The one to the north, the Generalife Watchtower, comprises five graceful, stylish archways and in the rear, three others of marble, with stalactite capitals. Another room offers a fine view of Grenada's three hills: Albaicin, Sacromonte and Alhambra. Charles V had a palace built on the Alhambra: square in shape, with a large, handsome, circular courtyard. With this building he affirmed the victory that was the Reconquista, and all the splendor of the Spanish Renaissance.

Above
Grenada: the Fountain of the Lions

These twelve stone lions have given their name to an entire section of the Alhambra. For the Arabs, people accustomed to a hot climate, shade and coolness were part of the art of living and a sign of wealth. The more powerful the master of the house, the more elegant and refreshing his patio. And as the Prophet Mohamed remarked, the sound of flowing water is an echo of Paradise.

Facing page
The Courtyard of the Lions

This stunning demonstration of aesthetic sensitivity was, one might say, the Arabs' farewell gesture to Spain. The last dynasty, the Nasrids, was much more taken with civic than religious art, as the magnificent stucco work in the Courtyard of the Lions illustrates. A palace as sophisticated as this one is a far cry from the early Muslim architecture that gave us, for example, the forest of columns in the mosque in Cordoba.

Italy

The Grand Canal at Santa Maria della Salute

To ward off the Black Plague in 1630, Venice decided to build a church in honor of the Virgin Mary. The architect of this Baroque masterpiece, begun in 1631, was Baldassare Longhena. To protect the ground the church was to be built on, more than a million piles had to be sunk. The church of Santa Maria della Salute was finally consecrated in 1687, five years after Longhena's death. Every year on 21 November, a bridge of boats is created to allow a commemorative procession to cross the Grand Canal.

Venice was founded in the 6th century by the inhabitants of the Roman province of Venetia, who were in flight from the Lombards and seeking refuge on the small islands in the lagoons. They remained under the tutelage of the Byzantine exarch of Ravenna. In the 8th century a dux ("leader" in Latin) or doge (in Venetian) was elected and the Byzantine influence lessened. Venice began to grow from the island of Rivo Alto or "Rialto". Made up of 118 islands, the archipelago had as its main thoroughfare the Grand Canal, together with 177 smaller canals, the rii, and 450 bridges. The houses and palaces were built on piles. Venice's prosperity grew out of its role as a commercial go-between for East and West.

Precious metals, spices, silk, sheets, wood and slaves were bought in Constantinople, Alexandria and the Balkans and resold in Western Europe.

Completed in 1094, the basilica of St Mark is a splendid combination of Roman and Byzantine art. It is home to relics said to be those of St Mark the Evangelist, the city's patron saint. In those days Venice was an aristocratic republic whose Doges were recruited from a handful of prominent property-owning families who invested in sea-trading operations. The Venetians took over the Dalmatian coast from Zara (Zadar) to Ragusa (Dubrovnik). In 1204 they joined the Crusaders in the pillaging of Constantinople and established a colonial empire in the Greek islands, the Peloponnesus

and Salonika. They were the owners of Christendom's largest sea-going fleet. In 1295 Marco Polo, son of a Venetian merchant, returned from an expedition to distant China, but was captured and imprisoned by the Genoese. In the depths of his dungeon he recounted to a fellow-prisoner the fabulous voyage we now know as the book The Travels of Marco Polo.

The Doge's power was held in check by a Great Council of 1000 members and the Council of Ten. After four separate wars with Genoa, Venice emerged victorious and via the conquests of its mercenary warlords – the condottieri – extended its territory onto dry land in northern Italy. However, the capture of Constantinople by the Turks in 1453, the discovery of America by Christopher Columbus in 1492 and the arrival of Vasco da Gama in India seriously damaged the Venetian monopoly of pepper and spices. Venice adapted to the new situation,

became Europe's leading distribution centre and developed new activities as well: banking, ship-building, wool working, glass making and luxury handmade goods.The Rialto Bridge was rebuilt in marble. The ducal palace (residence of the Doges and the Councils), the Procurator's House, the Clocktower and the spectacular palaces along the Grand Canal all bore witness to Venice's grandeur. But in spite of the sumptuous celebrations – the carnival and the election of the Doge – and the genius of its painters, Venice began to decline. The Turks seized Cyprus and Crete and after conquering the city in 1797, Napoleon Bonaparte handed it over to Austria. In 1866 the residents voted to join the Kingdom of Italy. Despite floods, pollution and a shrinking population, Venice remains a luminous city, with its bricks and tiles, its marble and its gold. Of its days of glory it has retained a very special aura and a truly exceptional beauty.

The Canal San Marco at the Doges' Palace

In the 9th century the Doges built a palace as their seat of power and a meeting place for the Councils. Since the time of that first, Byzantine building, the Doges' Palace has been destroyed by fire several times. The current palace was begun in 1340; the facade giving onto the lagoon was finished in 1404 and the one on the Piazzetta in 1424. The latter was re-created identically after the fire of 1577 – an incomparable example of the Flamboyant Gothic style. The Grand Council chamber can hold several thousand people.

Albania

Despite its closeness to Europe, Albania remains one of the world's least-known countries. This narrow strip of mountainous terrain totaling 30,000 square kilometers (19,000 square miles) faces southeastern Italy. Its neighbors are Montenegro and Macedonia, and to the south, Greece and the island of Corfu. Albania's relationships with its neighbors have always been stormy and for a long period of Communist rule it traded solely with distant China – or, to be more exact, it received aid from that country.

Albania was first settled in paleolithic times. During the thousand years before the birth of Jesus it prospered on the western border of the kingdom of Illyria, which extended as far as the Danube.

The main source of its wealth was farming and today, as twenty-five centuries ago, it remains a basically agricultural country.

In the 7th century BC, the Greeks arrived. The sites of Apollonia, Epidamnos (later Durrës), Butrint and many others are testimony to this Greco-Illyrian period. The Greeks were followed by the Romans, who built the Via Egnatia across the country, linking Rome to Byzantium.

In the 2nd century BC the whole of Illyria became Roman and a century later Julius Caesar sent colonists there to reinforce Rome's hold. Illyria gave Rome three emperors: Aurelius, Diocletian and Constantine. The region was then taken over by Byzantium, but was later plundered by the Barbarians – who in turn were followed by the Slavs. The territory was split into north and south, with the southern population putting up fierce resistance and keeping a considerable amount of local power for themselves.

In the 9th century Albania fell into the hands of the Bulgarian kings, who had recently converted to Christianity. The people did not take to their new masters at all – nor, in the 11th century, to attempts at invasion by the Vikings and the Crusaders. In the late 13th century Charles of Anjou, brother of the saintly King Louis IX of France, had himself proclaimed King of Albania, but local tensions quickly forced him from the throne.

Apollonia

Situated 10 kilometers (6 miles) from the coast, at the watershed between the Adriatic and Ionian seas, Apollonia seems to have been inhabited since prehistoric times. Like Butrint, this was an Illyrian city. With the coming of colonists from Corinth and nearby Corfu, the Greeks dedicated the site to Apollo. Here we see the remains of his temple.

The next takeover attempt was by Serbia, but organized resistance came from the feudal lords and mountain people; unfortunately they were unable to agree among themselves and finally the region was taken by the Turks – closely observed, however, by the Venetians, whose interests were more economic than religious.

It was at this time that Skanderbeg, the great Albanian hero made his appearance. Son of a princely family that had been humiliated by the Turks, as a child he had been handed over to the enemy as a hostage. His hatred of the Turks embodied all the rebellious passion of the Albanian people. Taking advantage of a moment when the Turks were having trouble with the Hungarians – Albania's allies – he captured the citadel at Kruja, which at once became the symbol of Albanian resistance. From one of its windows he hung his family's flag with its double-headed eagle – now the national emblem – and proclaimed his country's independence. This generated such enthusiasm that he was able to raise an army of volunteers.

Worried by the idea that this movement might threaten their trading centers in Albania, the Venetians joined forces with the Turks to overthrow Skanderbeg. The hero was conquered after resisting ferociously, but the Venetians lost out too, as the Turks now became sole masters of the country – until the second half of the 19th century. Thus Albania lived for five hundred years under the Turkish yoke, but in the interests of all concerned the Pashas strove to keep the economy healthy. In the 19th century, as elsewhere, the winds of nationalism began blowing through Albania, but this small, feudal state never attracted the same sympathy as the Greeks and never produced a leader as charismatic as d'Annunzio in Italy.

Finally, in 1912, Albania achieved independence, but under a king whose reign was to last barely a year. In 1914 the Austrians and Italians carved the country up between them, but Albania regained its independence in 1919, and a young chief, Ahmet Zogu, became ruler by somewhat dubious means.

In 1928 Zogu became King Zog I. He quickly, if somewhat unwillingly, formed an alliance with the Italians, who then invaded Albania and incorporated it into fascist Italy under King Victor Emmanuel. The resistance movement that sprang up was run by the French-educated communist Enver Hoxha, who was to govern the country until his death in 1985. Faithful to the tradition of Albanian isolationism, he provoked conflict with all his country's neighbors.

Skanderbeg's fort

This is the rebuilt 15th-century fort at Kruja, 20 kilometers north of the capital, Tirana. It was from here that Skanderbeg organized resistance to the Turks..

Greece: Athens

For many of us the silhouette of the Parthenon on the heights of the Acropolis symbolizes Greece's role as the cradle of Western civilization. A crucial period in human history had its beginnings on this rocky outcrop.

The story of Athens begins at the close of the Neolithic, with the arrival of the Pelasgians. They were, however, soon ousted by the Ionians, a people who can be considered, so to speak, the first Greeks: their language provided the basis of classical Greek. They established a dozen city-states, among them Cecropia, which would later become Athens. Here ruled Cecrops, the first Athenian king, who outlawed human sacrifice and taught the people both writing and farming. Cecrops also offered the West its first social institutions. His successor, the priest-king Erectheus, built Athens' first temple. Then came the Achaeans, who mainly settled in the Peloponnesus, with Mycenae as their major kingdom. Mycenae was in close contact with the much more highly evolved civilization in Crete. Many Greek cities possessed an acropolis, but the Acropolis has always been the one in Athens, a city that went on to become the capital of a kingdom. A palace was built on the Acropolis and Athenian civilization would reach its high point – and its downfall – with the Trojan war.

The great hero of this era was Theseus, son of Aegeus, a young prince who freed Greece's cities from the tribute exacted by the hideous Minotaur, a creature half-man, half-bull living in a labyrinth in Crete. To appease its appetite the Minotaur demanded an offering of seven young men and seven young women. It is to Theseus that we owe the unification of early Greece, with Athens as its capital. Dividing the population into three classes – nobles, tradesmen and farmers – he set up the first democratic institutions and created the first agora or public meeting place at the foot of the Acropolis. When the Dorian invasion came, Athens was saved by King Kodros (or Codrus), who obeyed a prediction requiring him to have himself killed by the enemy. This marked the end of the Athenian monarchy, nobody being regarded as a worthy successor to such a ruler. Athens continued to prosper during the three centuries of the "geometric era", although the wealth was mainly

accumulated by the Eupatrides ("well-born"), who were sometimes in conflict with the people. When Draco set out to put an end to these quarrels, he gave Athens its first written laws – laws so stringent they were said to have been written in blood.

Born into a poor but aristocratic family, Solon made his fortune as a trader traveling far and wide. Highly respected, he returned from his voyages to an Athens where the aristocracy was torn by disputes and exploiting the people. The state was weak and did not dare reclaim the island of Salamina from the Megarians. Appointed archon – chief magistrate – in 594 BC, Solon proclaimed the first "democratic" constitution, withdrawing the nobility's privileges and requiring citizens to serve society according to their financial means. Among the measures attributed to him are land reform, the basis of fiscal law, property law and a people's court. Once his constitution had gone into effect, he set off on his travels again. On his return he found Pisistratus seeking to calm the people by offering entertainment in the form of organized festivities and the first performances of Greek tragedy in Athens. Pisistratus was also continuing the town planning work begun by Solon. The Acropolis took on a new role: no longer was it a citadel, a refuge for the people when the Persians attacked; it became a sacred site, covered with temples. At the foot of the Acropolis Athens too was dotted with monuments.

In 508 BC Clisthenes founded what was truly Athenian democracy. He divided Attica into 10 demes and increased the number of council members to 500. Many people were now entitled to the rank of full citizen and the enthusiastic Athenians drove the Persians back at Marathon. However, when the Persians returned yet again, the Athenians were forced to abandon their city and it was burnt to the ground. Not to be discouraged, Themistocles lay in wait for the Persian fleet off Salamina (480 BC) and won a crushing victory. At last Athenian supremacy was complete, on land and sea. Athens organized a defensive confederation, the League of Delos, and deciding that the League's treasure would be better off inside the city walls, organized the enormous celebrations known as the Panathenaea. This was Athens at the height of its splendor under Pericles.

Bassae

At Bassae we find ourselves in a relatively unknown Greece. This shrine is probably one of the last vestiges of Athenian influence in the Peloponnesus, of the time before austere, militaristic Sparta wiped out the city that preferred the arts and sciences to the sword.

The history of the peopling of the Peloponnesus is in many ways similar to that of Attica, its neighbor to the north, but a fundamental difference lies in the period at which each achieved its high point: the Mycenaean civilization was almost a thousand years older than its Athenian equivalent. The Peloponnesus took wing under the influence of the Achaeans, who were to be savagely brought low by the Dorians. Argos and Pylos were razed to the ground, leaving only the cyclopean fortresses at Tiryns, the walls of Mycenae, the Gate of Lions and the famous tomb of Agamemnon, together with the golden mask attributed to him by Schliemann.

For an idea of the lost Achaean palaces and the doomed family of the Atrides, we must turn to the writings of Homer, Aeschylus, Sophocles and Euripides. The Mycenaean civilization is better known through the Trojan War and the deeds of Achilles, Agamemnon, Helen, Clytemnestra, Orestes and Electra, than through any contact it might have had with its neighbors. Once the Dorians had put paid to the Achaeans, they established new centers like Corinth and Sparta, homes to a sea-going ruling class.

The sheer violence of the Atrides makes it difficult to imagine that their ancestors had been civilized by contact with the delicate Cretans. And yet, if we exclude the Atrides, there was an atmosphere in the Peloponnesus that could be most agreeable. True, the coasts were ravaged by the wind, but even at the foot of the acropolises of Mycenae and Tiryns there were fragrant olive groves where daily life had nothing oppressive about it.

The Crusaders who dotted their narrow fortresses over the southern Peloponnesus had fallen under the spell of the kingdom they called Morea. The site of Mistra offers a charming evocation of Greece in those Frankish times.

The temple of Apollo Epikouros

The countryside around Bassae is as rugged and mountainous as any in Europe. Set at 1100 meters (3600 ft) above sea level, this temple offers a moving intimation of the faith of the peoples that Christians dismissed as pagans. The temple at Bassae was dedicated to Apollo Epikouros ("Apollo the Helpful") by the inhabitants of the nearby town of Phygalia to thank the gods for saving them from the plague. One of the best preserved temples in the Greek world, it was doubtless partly designed by Ictinos, responsible for the Parthenon. Built of local limestone, it is unusual in that it faces north. It offers an interesting mix of the three Greek orders: Doric columns outside, Ionian columns inside and, in the inner chamber or naos, a single Corinthian column which is perhaps the most ancient of its kind. On this isolated site, not far from towns that have never lost the medieval atmosphere of Balkan mountain villages, there is nothing to suggest that only a few dozen miles away Olympia and Epidaurus offer sun-drenched strolls through their countless ruins: here temples, theatres, stadiums, tholoi (dome-shaped tombs), statues and ex-votos conjure up all the sophistication of this civilization.

Czechie

The Rue de Paris

This view shows only a tiny part of the roofs of Prague – and relatively modern ones, along the Rue de Paris, the great thoroughfare created after the demolition of the ghetto in the closing years of the 19th century. In the background is the belltower housing the famous astronomical clock, together with the Town Hall and the church of St Nicholas.

The Charles Bridge and the castle

The Charles Bridge is often considered the historical heart of Prague. Built in 1367-83, it is 516 meters (1700 ft) long and 10 meters (33 ft) wide. The thirty statues are in fact copies of works by the famous 17th-century sculptor Matthias Braun. High up loom the castle and St Guy's cathedral; begun under Charles IV in 1344, the latter was only finished in 1933.

The first Slavs moved onto the hills of Prague overlooking a ford on the river Vltava – pra means "threshold" – somewhere around the 5th century.

In 1257 the ruling Premyslide dynasty was subjugated by the Germanic Empire, with the Czechs doing all they could to resist German influence.

When Karl IV became emperor in 1355, Prague began a period of enormous commercial and artistic expansion. In 1419 the Hussites – disciples of religious reformer Jan Hus, who had been burnt at the stake in 1415 – killed King Wenceslas IV's Catholic councilors by throwing them from a high window. Nonetheless, the Catholic monarchy emerged victorious and Bohemia became part of the Austrian states ruled by the Hapsburgs. As building went ahead during the Renaissance, Prague became steadily more beautiful; and the Catholic victory at the battle of White Mountain (1620) was reflected in the palaces and Baroque churches of the counter-Reformation.

Prague was now famous as the "Golden City". In the 18th century Joseph II formed its four districts into a single unit: Hradcany (the castle area), Mala Strana ("Lesser Quarter"), Stare Mesto ("Old Town") and Nové Mesto ("New Town"). Situated on the hill on the left bank of the river, Hradcany is the royal district, with a Gothic castle that was modernized in the 18th century. Every architectural style can be found in Hradcany: Romanesque at St George's basilica, Flamboyant Gothic at St Guy's cathedral, Renaissance at the Schwartzenberg Palace, Rococo at the bishop's palace and, especially, Baroque at the Cernin Palace, the shrine of Our Lady of Loreto and the Strahov monastery.

The Baroque is also to be found in Mala Strana: the palace of the Knights of Malta, the churches of St Thomas and Our Lady of Victories, and the Wallenstein palace. More than 500 meters (1650 ft) long, the Charles Bridge is a Gothic structure of powerfully beautiful arches, adorned with 30 large Baroque statues. Dominated by the Gothic spires and turrets of the church of Our Lady of Tin, Old Town Square is bright with harmonious colors and every hour sees people waiting for the astronomical clock to chime at the Town Hall. Prague is also famed as the home of writers Franz Kafka and Rainer Maria Rilke.

Russia: Moscow

The capital of the Tsars and the Russian Orthodox Church – one of its nicknames is "the Third Rome" – Moscow has been in a state of upheaval since the dramatic political changes of the late 1980s and the 1990s.

The USSR no longer exists: Russia has become an independent republic and a founder member of the Commonwealth of Independent States (CIS).

Gone is the talk of a "world socialist revolution", of "socialism in one country" and of "the capital of the socialist bloc": now the issues are the "shift to a market economy" and "rampant capitalism".

Situated on the banks of the Moskova, between the Don and Volga basins at the centre of the great Russian plain, Moscow was a historical unknown until 1147, when the annals mention it as a fishing village. Nonetheless it was here, in 1156, that Yuri Dolgoruki, a descendant of the Norse chieftain Rurik, built the wooden palisade for his first fortress or kreml – whence the name Kremlin. However the town was devastated by the princes of Riazan in 1176 and by the Tartars in 1237.

The capture of Kiev by the Mongol invaders in 1240 gave Moscow the opportunity to take on a broader historical role. Tsar Ivan I Kalita decided to make the city his political and religious capital in 1328 and built the Cathedral of the Assumption – Uspensky Sobor – there.

The Tartars were defeated at Kulikovo ("field of the woodcocks") by Dimitri Donskoi in 1380.

On the banks of the Moskova

Behind the walls of the Kremlin, a sort of triangle two kilometers (1.25 miles) long, lies an incredible profusion of architectural works of art: the Great Palace, the Cathedral of the Archangel and the Great Belltower. Behind the belltower is the Cathedral of the Assumption, built by the Bolognese architect Fioravanti for Ivan III in 1475-79.

In the 16th century Vassily III called in Italian architects to build the cathedrals of the Kremlin; and European merchants, Germans in particular, moved into the districts of Kitai Gorod ("the Chinese City") and Belyi Gorod ("the White City").

Ivan IV – "the Terrible" – crushed the revolt of the Boyars, leaders of the Russian nobility, drove the Tartars back into the Crimea and set out to conquer Siberia.

Under the flag of a false Tsar passing himself off as Dimitri, the (late!) son of Ivan the Terrible, the Poles took Moscow and it was not until 1612 that a revolt led by Minin, a butcher, and Prince Pojarski forced the Catholic invaders out in the name of Russian orthodoxy.

With the coming of Mikhail Romanov, elected Tsar in 1613, a new dynasty was born. In 1712 Peter the Great, who detested Moscow, had no hesitation about moving the capital to St Petersburg, close to the Baltic and looking towards the West.

Tsars and Tsarinas continued to be crowned in Moscow, but otherwise abandoned the city to the merchant classes. Napoleon Bonaparte's army took Moscow in 1812, but was forced to withdraw when the people set a fire that destroyed, in all, three-quarters of the city's housing.

The superb palace of the Kremlin was rebuilt in 1839, followed by the whole of the old city. New districts continued to be created as Moscow expanded. The revolution of 1905 was put down; that of 1917 succeeded, but only after drawn-out battles.

On 12 March 1918 the new Soviet government declared Moscow the capital again – a means of protecting the country against any future threat from the German army. In 1941 Hitler's Wehrmacht was turned back only 30 kilometers (19 miles) from the city. Moscow then had to live through the dark years of Communism, a brutal regime whose sudden collapse was proof that expert opinion is not always infallible.

St Petersburg

After his victory over Sweden, Tsar Peter the Great decided it was time to assert the presence of the Russian empire on the Baltic and open the country up to Western European influences. So he ordered the building of the Peter and Paul Fortress on an island in the river Neva, following this up with the Admiralty and Kronstadt fortresses.

For these projects he used foreign architects: the Swiss Domenico Trezzi for the Peter and Paul Fortress and the Alexander Nevski monastery; and Frenchman Jean-Baptiste Leblond whose plan for the new city, including the Nevski Prospect, was based on Versailles.

The Tsar had no hesitation about using hundreds of thousands of men – soldiers, Swedish and Turkish prisoners, Finnish and Estonian deportees – to sink piles into the mud of the marshland and transport the stone for the buildings. By decree he called in population groups from all over the empire, banned all building elsewhere in stone and forced every landowner with more than 500 serfs to build a two-story stone house in the new city.

It was this thoroughly authoritarian approach that made St Petersburg the most beautiful city in Russia – and, in 1712, its new capital. Taking over from Moscow, St Petersburg was soon a rival for Venice, Amsterdam and Paris, a brilliant showcase for an empire bent on taking advantage of the latest advances in the West. Yet it could not hide the reality of an enormous, backward country caught somewhere between Europe and Asia. Tsarina Elizabeth, daughter of Peter the Great, commissioned the Italian architect Rastrelli to build Catherine's Palace at Tsarskoye Selo (1756) and the Winter Palace (1762), both masterpieces of Russian Baroque. She also added extensions to Petrodvorets, the Versailles Palace of the Tsars. Catherine II adopted the neo-Classical style, adding the Little Hermitage to the Winter Palace, and building the Hermitage Theatre and the Alexander and Tauride Palaces.

The Kazan Cathedral was built under Alexander I and St Isaac's Cathedral under Alexander II.

St Petersburg became Petrograd in 1914 and Leningrad in 1924. In 1991 residents decided by referendum to return to their city's original name.

Catherine's Palace

This sumptuous palace stands at not far from St Petersburg at Tsarskoye Selo ("the Tsar's village"), renamed Pushkin by the revolutionaries: Russia's famous poet had studied at the Imperial school there. The palace was named after Catherine I, wife of Peter the Great and his successor in the two years following his death. When her spouse offered her this vast domain, she set about arranging it to her taste even before the architect Rastrelli had built the 300 meter (1000 ft) long palace.

Turkey

The history of Turkey goes back three to four thousand years. After the Hittite empire Anatolia, in Asia Minor, was successively part of the Greek, Roman, Byzantine and Ottoman civilizations.

The Greeks arrived in 1000 BC, leaving us the historic sites of Miletos, Ephesus, Samos, Priena, Pergamum and Troy. Byzantium was founded on the Bosphorus in the 7th century BC.

Then Anatolia was taken over by the Romans. Constantine the Great (324-337 AD) brought unity to the Roman Empire, converted to Christianity and founded a new capital, Constantinople – a second Rome – on the site of Byzantium. Thus was born the Eastern Roman Empire, later the Byzantine Empire.

Byzantium's high point came with the rule of the emperor Justinian (527-565). He put up lavish religious buildings, among them the splendid basilica of Saint Sophia (Haghia Sophia), a masterpiece of Byzantine architecture consecrated on 26 December 537.

Today's St Sophia is a curious mix: an initially Christian place of worship transformed into a celebrated mosque. Under its magnificent central dome, with its mosaic ornamentation, are four enormous panels bearing quotations from the Koran.

Turkish nomads, originally from Central Asia, had spread throughout Asia Minor. Constantine XI Paleologus, the last emperor of the Eastern Empire, fell in battle against another Turkish dynasty, the Ottomans, in 1453. This was the end of the Eastern Roman Empire.

Mehmet II the Conqueror (1451-1481) made Constantinople an Islamic capital, changing its name to Istanbul and building mosques, palaces – among them the famous Topkapi – and fountains.

Known as the Blue Mosque, the mosque of Sultan Ahmet I is unquestionably the most beautiful in all Istanbul. Built between 1609 and 1616, its walls covered with magnificent tiling, it rises superbly opposite St Sophia. It was under Sulieman I the Magnificent (1520-1566) that the Ottoman Empire underwent its greatest period of expansion.

Despite the decline of the Empire, Istanbul has never lost its fascination. Today's capital is Ankara, but it is still Istanbul, a symbolic crossroads between East and West, that draws visitors from all over the world.

St Sophia

A Christian basilica for over 900 years, then a mosque for almost 500 years, St Sophia has been a museum since 1935. Thought to have been built by the Emperor Constantine in the 4th century, the building was twice destroyed by fire before being rebuilt as we know it today by the Emperor Justinian, two hundred years later. The dome is 55 meters (180 ft) high and 30 meters (100 ft) in diameter. Among St Sophia's many remarkable features are fine Byzantine mosaics.

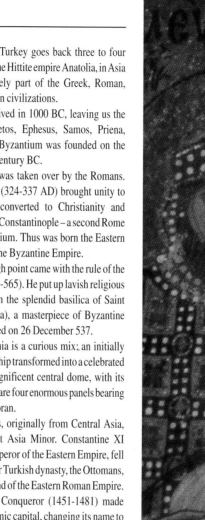

Lebanon

We decided to open the section on Asia with the Roman ruins at Baalbek for two reasons. Firstly, Lebanon is very close to Europe; and secondly, for almost three thousand years before the birth of Christ, this was an extremely prosperous country. A long strip of land running down the east coast of the Mediterranean, Lebanon was a maritime and trade outlet for many different Asian countries. First came the Cananeans, whose ancestor Canaan was the grandson of Noah and the son of Ham. They were followed by the Phoenicians, the greatest trading power of all antiquity: their city-states competed with each other, but joined forces the moment an enemy appeared. The main cities were Biblos, Sidon and Tyre; the Greek historian Herodotus situates the founding of Tyre at 2750 BC. The Phoenicians soon came to dominate the Mediterranean, their most important trading partner being Egypt.

The invasion of the Hyksos reversed the situation. The Egyptians finally defeated them and then subjugated Phoenicia, which nonetheless continued to develop: it was at this time that the Phoenician alphabet was born. Weakened by internal conflict, Egypt was unable to prevent the Phoenicians from regaining their independence, and now a single city – Tyre – dominated all the others. Phoenician mariners set up trading posts all over the Mediterranean and on the Atlantic as well.

Becoming more powerful, Assyria needed a sea outlet and Phoenicia, rather than suffer the consequences of war, bought a peace treaty from Salmanazar III. Nonetheless the Assyrians behaved as despots and Dido, a princess of Tyre set out westwards to found Kart-Hadasht ("new city") near the colony of Utica. This spelled the end of the Phoenician empire and the rise of Carthage.

Only with the coming of the Romans did the Phoenicians regain their old influence. Dedicated to Jupiter, the cities of Biblos, Tyre, Beryte (the future Beirut) and Baalbek (renamed Heliopolis) entered on a phase of great prosperity. However, the end of the "Pax Romana" brought a fresh series of invasions. More or less Christian since St Paul's time, Lebanon was conquered in the 7th century by the Arabs, but after a long period of internal struggle became Christian again under the Franks. The latter were driven out by the Mamelukes from Egypt, who were themselves removed by the Ottomans in 1516. In 1860 the Muslim Druzes began threatening the Christians and Napoleon III sent in an expeditionary force. In 1926 Lebanon became a republic and the Lebanese people enjoyed economic development reminiscent of that of their Phoenician ancestors. Unfortunately 1975 saw the country in the thick of conflict in the Near East.

Facing page
Baalbek: the temple of Jupiter
In this ancient city where the Phoenicians had worshiped Baal, the Romans raised an enormous temple to Jupiter, master of all the gods. The entry to the temple was very striking, the steps leading to it being as wide as the building itself. Today, all that remains to bear witness to this gigantic tribute are these 6 columns, each 20 meters (66 ft) high and 2.2 meters (7 ft) in diameter.

Above
The temple of Bacchus
This shrine is remarkably well preserved, but the name it bears is somewhat approximate, being based on the presence of statues of Bacchus, god of wine. It would seem, in fact, that this was a kind of all-purpose temple, for gods including Baal, Venus, Mercury and Bacchus.

Israel

Deep in the mountains of Judea, in a countryside of greens and mauves and pinks, Jerusalem mingles synagogues, mosques and churches. For millions of Christians all over the world this is the site of the Holy Sepulcher, the burial place of Christ. This "Holy Land" extends to the far end of the fertile crescent between the river Jordan and the Mediterranean. The name Jerusalem is said to derive from Shalem, a god of the Semitic people the Amorites, and in Hebrew means "peace will come".

The city's history is all too accurate a reflection of the frictions between the three great monotheist religions: Judaism, Islam and Christianity.

It was around the 16th century BC that the Hebrews, a people from Chaldea, settled in the land of Canaan. Some of them continued on as far as Egypt, where they were enslaved by the Pharaohs. It is at this point that history and the Biblical accounts begin to complement each other. At the end of the 13th century BC, Moses, charged with a divine mission, led the Hebrews to the promised land of he had seen in a vision: the land of the Cananeans. The Bible recounts their exodus from Egypt and their time in the wilderness.

Divided up into tribes, the Hebrews settled on the shores of the Dead Sea. Around 1000 BC one group, the Israelites, chose its first king, Saul, whose successor, David, soon made Jerusalem his capital.

The city was home to the Ark of the Covenant, in which were the Tables of the Law, entrusted to Moses by Jehovah. David's son Solomon (975-935 BC) used 150,000 workers to build the Temple of the world's first monotheist religions. Famed for his wisdom, this ruler had a considerable influence on the Islamic tradition, under the name Sulieman.

In 587 BC Jerusalem was razed by Nabuchad-nezzar and its people deported to Babylon. In 538 BC the Persian king Cyrus gave permission for the Jewish people to return and to rebuild their city and the Temple.

After the conquest by Alexander the Great, the Maccabees organized a rebellion against their Greek occupiers and founded the dynasty of the Asmoneans. After Pompey took Jerusalem by storm in 63 BC, King Herod I, an ally of the Romans, rebuilt the Temple, giving it all the splendor of the Temple of Solomon. There now remain only the foundations: the enormous blocks of stone of the Wailing Wall, where Jews come to meditate and pray.

Deriving from Judaism, the new monotheist religion – Christianity – began to make headway, asserting its universality by seeking converts among non-Jewish peoples. For the Christians too, Jerusalem, scene of the Passion of Christ, was the Holy City.

Solomon's Arch

In the Negev desert, where Solomon had his copper and tin mines, erosion creates its own strange architectures. Three "works" stand out: the giant red "pillars", the astonishing, mushroom-shaped "table" and "Solomon's Arch", shown here.

Below
Jerusalem

This view of the former capital of Solomon sums up all the divisions created by the attachment felt for this place by the three monotheist religions: the gilded domes of the Russian Orthodox church, the crenellated wall of Sulieman the Magnificent and the Dome of the Rock, from which Mahomet was raised to Heaven.

When the Jews rose against Rome in 66 AD, the emperor Titus destroyed Jerusalem. In 135 it was razed again by Hadrian, who built a new city, Aelia Capitolina on the site and put it off limits to Jews. In 326 Constantine confirmed the victory of Christianity, built the Church of the Holy Sepulcher and turned Jerusalem into a place of pilgrimage for the Roman Empire's new official religion. The city's Byzantine period is attested by the crypt of the church of St John the Baptist, St George's Chapel and the church of St Stephen.

With the Arab conquest in 638, a third monotheist religion, Islam, also declared Jerusalem its holy city ("Al-Quds"). The gilded Dome of the Rock harks back to the sacrifice of Isaac by Abraham and the site from which Mahomet was taken up to Heaven. The more recent Al-Aqsa Mosque has been remodeled several times and a silver dome added.

Rebuilt in the 12th century, at the time of the Crusades and the Latin Kingdom of Jerusalem (1099-1244), the Church of the Holy Sepulcher is shared by different Christian persuasions: Greek Orthodox, Roman Catholic, Armenian, Coptic and others. Divided in two when Israel was founded in 1948, Jerusalem became entirely Israeli in 1967.

The Wailing Wall

Built with the foundation stones of the Temple of Solomon, this wall is the ultimate symbol of the Jewish people's attachment to Jerusalem.

Iran

Few ruined sites are as evocative as that of Persepolis. This was the ancient capital of the Achaemenids, the powerful dynasty that founded the Persian empire, the largest in all antiquity. At the height of its glory the empire's territory extended from the Indus Valley in the east to Thrace in the west.

At the beginning of the 5th century BC Darius, king of Persia, decided to build a capital worthy of his power. Calling in the empire's most accomplished artists and craftsmen, he created Persepolis, the "city of the Persians".

Many alterations were effected by his successor, Xerxes I, who also completed projects left unfinished under Darius. But then, recounts Plutarch, after a night of orgiastic celebrations, Alexander the Great set the city on fire, leaving nothing but a wasteland of ruins. Persepolis stood for only two hundred years, but such was its splendor that even today it still symbolizes all the magnificence and refinement of antiquity.

Situated on the Marvdasht plain in present-day Iran, the site of Persepolis still bears the traces of the enormous earth-moving and engineering processes required by its building. This royal residential complex was a sumptuously monumental affair whose ceremonial staircase was so wide that it could readily

be climbed on horseback. On different sides Xerxes' gate, guarded by two winged bulls, and the monumental gate lead to different buildings of which the main ones are the palaces of Darius and Xerxes, the Hall of a Hundred Columns and the Apadana palace complex. It was here that the sovereigns received the tribute brought by their subject peoples, in a setting that left no doubt as to the prestige and sheer power of the Empire.

It is said that on New Year's Day – the Day of Noruz, dedicated to Ahura Mazda, the god of light – the celebrations were such that processions from twenty-eight different nations came to the throne, bringing the king presents from all over the known world. These ceremonies are portrayed in some of the low-relief sculptures on the walls of Persepolis: the processions are led by the Medes and Persians, followed by delegations from Libya, Egypt, Ethiopia and many other countries.

Yet today, of all the splendor that made Persepolis one of antiquity's most remarkable cities, only a few sculptures and buildings remain as testimony to the might of the Achaemenids. The restoration of Persepolis was carried out under the Shah of Iran in the 1970s.

Central Asia

Facing page

Bukhara: Chor Minor

With its four minarets ("chor minor") and crane's nest, this 19th-century school in Bukhara is the emblem of the city.

Below

Khiva: Kunya Ark

Khiva is unique: a Muslim museum city of civil, religious and military buildings. Here we see the entry to the Kunya Ark citadel.

Different civilizations developed in Central Asia, where tribes of nomads and shepherds often continued to lead lives running counter to the current of history.

In the 6th and 7th centuries Turkish and Arab tribes swept through the region, forcing those they conquered to convert to Islam and doing away with the religions already in place: Buddhism, Zoroastrianism and the Nestorian and Manichean variants of Christianity. The period between the 9th and 15th centuries brought dominance by a succession of feudal states. The Persian Samanide dynasty (819-999) took over Transoxiana and Khorasan, while turning Samarkand and their capital city of Bukhara into focal points for art and culture. In the 11th and 12th centuries the Turkish dynasty of the Seljukids took over Bukhara and a vast area around the city. The Khorezmians were a separate, independent Muslim dynasty from the banks of the Amou-Daria river in Turkestan.

The 13th century saw the nomadic Mongols leave the steppes of their native Mongolia and set out to conquer an enormous empire. Led by Genghis Khan, these ferocious horsemen overthrew every kingdom they encountered as they advanced westwards, in company with Turkish tribesmen. The Mongol religion was a form of ancestral shamanism, but their forays brought them into contact with three great religions: Buddhism, Islam and Christianity.

The Mongol prince Temujin became the greatest conqueror in all of history. After subduing all the neighboring tribes he had himself proclaimed Genghis Khan ("Universal Ruler") in 1206 and governed the Mongols under that name. At the head of an army of 20,000 men, he began building an empire which, at his death, stretched from the Pacific Ocean to western Asia. Cruel and pitiless, Genghis Khan was a masterly organizer and a mighty warrior who thought nothing of massacring entire populations and burning whole cities to the ground. His savage hordes were guilty of the worst imaginable atrocities. In 1211 the Mongols invaded northern China and when Peking fell in 1215 it was plundered and burnt.

In the period 1216-1223, the Muslim empire of Khorezm, situated along the Amou-Daria river in Turkestan, was wiped out. With his son Tolui, Genghis Khan reached Bukhara, then marched on Samarkand. The two cities were burnt to the ground and their people subjected to terrible violence. The artists and craftsmen were spared, but deported.

Other cities were besieged, emptied of their inhabitants and destroyed. At Merv, in 1221, the men, women and children were all decapitated. The invaders continued their bloodthirsty raids in the area around the Caspian sea and in Persia, Georgia, the Caucasus and the Crimea. Genghis Khan died during a campaign in China in 1227.

Above

**Samarkand:
the Chir Dor madrasa**

*The name comes from the two
tigers on the facade – a rare
example of illustration in
Muslim art. This is the most
imposing of the three madrasas
on the city's Registan Square.*

His successors continued to wreak havoc. His
four sons divided the empire between them and set out
on bloody expeditions against the Bulgars. In Russia
the population of Riazan was massacred, Moscow
sacked and Kiev destroyed in 1240. Batu Khan,
grandson of Genghis Khan and founder of the Golden
Horde in Russia around 1242, set about invading
Europe. In the mid-14th century Tamerlane – a
corruption of Timur Lang, meaning "Timur the Lame"

– brought the Mongol conquests to an end. His empire
stretched from southern Russia to Mongolia and from
northern India to Persia. A fanatical Muslim, Tamerlane banned all other religions and overthrew the Golden
Horde.

Samarkand became the capital of his empire and
the "rare pearl of the world". Tamerlane's grandson
Ulugbeg continued the building and embellishing of
caravan cities like Bukhara and Samarkand.

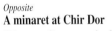

Opposite

A minaret at Chir Dor

This extraordinary example of mosaic evokes all the splendor of this mysterious city. Marakanda, the Greek city of the 6th century BC, became Arab in the 7th century AD. In the 14th century Tamerlane made it the luxurious capital of an empire dominated by Islam.

Facing page, bottom

Chir Dor (detail)

The pagans worshiped idols and their surroundings were full of images of their deities. Judaism allowed no images of Yahweh and several centuries passed before Christian churches began to portray Jesus and the saints. To distinguish itself from Christianity and assert a strength springing from austerity, Islam outlawed all human representation, even thought the Koran had forbidden only images of God. As a result, Muslim artists developed an extraordinary talent for portraying plant motifs and quotations from the Koran. Their most frequent materials were stone, marble and ceramic. Later the Persians, Mongols, Moguls and Ottomans took the Koran literally, excluding only the face of God from their superb paintings.

India :Taj Mahal

The Mogul empire in India was founded in 1526 by the emperor Babur, a descendant of Tamerlane and Genghis Khan. Between 1627 and 1658 Shah Jahn, the fifth emperor of the Great Mogul dynasty ruled over an empire stretching from the Himalayas in the north of India to Deccan in the south, and from Afghanistan and Baluchistan in the northwest to Bengal in the East.

His wife was called Mumtaz Mahal ("The Chosen One of the Palace") and Shah Jahan loved her very dearly, as events were to prove. She died in childbirth at the age of 37, after having had fourteen children, of whom seven survived. Griefstricken, Shah Jahan mourned her for two years, then decided to build the most exquisite mausoleum in the world as a tribute to her beauty and their love. The magnificent result was designed to stand up to the ravages of time and houses the graves of both Shah Jahn and his adored Mumtaz Mahal. In all the building process took sixteen years, from 1632 to 1648.

An absolute jewel, the colossal Taj Mahal at Agra is a masterpiece of majesty, symmetry and architectural lightness. The building was carried out by Persian and Ottoman architects, aided by twenty thousand workers and the most skilled craftsmen of the time, some of whom were brought in from Europe. The materials used came not only from India, but also from Persia, Russia and Tibet: white and black marble, semiprecious stones – opal, turquoise, sapphire and more – and red sandstone.

he overall composition of the building is delightfully harmonious, combining great purity and a near-mathematical exactness. The Taj includes the gardens, the entryway, the mausoleum and two similar, symmetrical buildings, one on each side: a mosque to the west aMeticulously divided up into squares and then into groups of four, the 17 hectares (40 acres) of gardens are very much in the Mogul tradition.

The gateway and the two buildings to the east and west combine red sandstone and white marble inlay. The gateway is elegantly ornamented with quotations from the Koran. Once inside, you discover the Taj Mahal in all its splendor. The mausoleum is set on a square terrace whose sides are 100 meters (330 ft); the square is made of pink sandstone and white marble, and at each corner stands a gleaming minaret of black-veined marble, forty meters (130 ft) high.

Eighteen meters (60 ft) in diameter, the enormous, graceful bulb of the dome is said to have been designed by Ismail Khan Rumi, who was perhaps a native of Constantinople. It is topped by a gilded pinnacle tapering into a spire that cuts through a crescent. The building itself is eight-sided – although the sides are not equal in length – and its total height is 62 meters (205 ft). The entire structure can be seen reflected in the waters of the pool, the channels and the river Yamuna, creating a truly striking perspective effect.

Readily recognized by people from the four corners of the earth, this masterpiece of Mogul elegance and refinement draws its inspiration from Persian architecture. Each facade of the tomb is identical, comprising a central iwan and four smaller ones to each side of it, on two levels. An iwan is a kind of room made of a pointed vault and open on one side.

Here the magnificent iwans are decorated with geometrical designs and floral patterns of semiprecious stones; they are made of white marble of Makrana, famed for the fineness of its texture. At the corners of the four facades are small pavilions, also octagonal in the Indian style and emphasizing and enhancing the overall unity of the Taj.

The interior of the tomb is decorated too, and in a way no visitor is ever likely to forget, such is the striking richness of its rooms and pavilions, and their finely carved marble ornamentation. Off the enormous central room, with its interior dome housing the cenotaphs of Mumtaz Mahal and Shah Jahn, are four small corner rooms.

The architecture of the Taj Mahal is a masterly blending of the Iranian, Central Asian and Indian raditions. Here in the world's most famous tomb we find superb ornamentation, perfect harmony of line, restraint, delicacy and sensitivity. This is the symbiosis of Muslim and Hindu culture for which the Moguls were striving: the world's most superb final resting place, in white marble.

Agra: the Taj Mahal

We owe this extraordinary marble tomb to the premature death of a sovereign's young wife. The very whiteness of the building echoes sorrow and pain: in the Muslim culture white is the color of mourning. Yet as we contemplate its beauty, we forget the suffering of the young ruler, losing ourselves in admiration of a masterpiece of Mogul art. Interestingly, its very whiteness provides a vivid contrast with the highly colored miniatures of which the Moguls were the unchallenged masters.

Khajuraho

The temples of Khajuraho were built near Madhya Pradesh in central India between the 9th and 11th centuries. Their makers were the Rajput sovereigns of the Chandela dynasty, who claimed to be the descendants of the moon god Chandra.

Of the original 85 temples, the 22 that have survived belong to the two main religions of medieval India: Hinduism and Jainism.

The art of the Chandela takes the form of a proliferation of sculptures both inside and outside these shrines. Among the gods portrayed with several sets of arms – a symbol of their multiple powers – are Vishnu, the protector; Shiva, the destroyer; and Surya, the sun god. At their sides dance the apsaras, adorably sensual nymphs, accompanied by more or less fantastic creatures. The famous "erotic" scenes of the mithuna – couples often shown intertwined in the act of love – astonished (when they did not shock) the first non-Indian visitors.

Today, however, it is accepted by all that these masterpieces are intended to accompany Tantric rites, in which the believer, with the assistance of a guru – a spiritual master – achieves transcendence through various techniques of physical and spiritual awakening. The beauty and sheer sensuality of the figures portrayed

on the walls and pillars of these temples also illustrate the basic tenet of Hindu philosophy: a mystical search for union with the universe.

The temples fall into three main groups: to the west, the east and the south. The western group is the largest and handsomest, notably including the Lakshmana temple dedicated to Vishnu and the Kandariya and Mahadeva temples dedicated to Shiva. To the east, around the village, stand three Hindu temples and four Jain shrines, including the striking Parshvanath temple, with its elegant sculptures and refined ornamentation. To the south we find the Duladeo and Chaturbhuja Hindu temples, dedicated to Shiva and Vishnu respectively.

All the Khajuraho temples possess a profound harmony between sculpture and architecture, a mingling of the sacred and the profane that ceaselessly reminds the viewer of the Hindu creation myth.

In this universe the Absolute, or Brahman, is represented by a head with three faces: that of Brahma, the creator of the world; of Vishnu, the protector and preserver, who intervenes in the affairs of men in the form of ten different "avatars"; and of Shiva, the destroyer. This is the Hindu trinity, symbol of the unity of the divine within the movement of the universe, of life and of death.

Above
The Lakshmana temple
This shrine is set on a terrace flanked by four temples. Dedicated to Vishnu, it owes its name to Lakshmi, goddess of good fortune and wife of Vishnu. Dating from the 10th century, it has the conical shape characteristic of Hindu temples.

Facing page
Detail of the Kandariya temple
These famous sculptures are part of the largest of all the Khajuraho temples, dedicated to Shiva. The sculptors have skilfully covered all available space on both the inside and outside of the temple, obedient to the Tantric doctrine of the period of the Chandelas: woman is the liberator of energy and sexual union is a vital step towards achieving union with the divinity.

Tibet

Known as the "Roof of the World" – among the Himalayas are valleys situated at 4000 meters (13,000 ft) above sea level – Tibet was long a totally unknown country.

The few attempts at conversion made by missionaries since the 17th century have left no trace. They were unable to enter the country other than singly or in pairs. When, in the early 20th century, the English sent in an expeditionary force of 600 to explore the trading possibilities, the Dalai Lama fled to Mongolia, but returned in 1912 and later met the only Western woman to have lived in Tibet: Alexandra David-Neel. On her return to Europe she published accounts of her travels, among them Mystics and Magicians of Tibet, but they were considered too "over the top" and failed to convince. In 1950 Communist China invaded Tibet and the West did nothing to prevent countless massacres. With the death of Mao in 1976, China began to open its borders – and those of Tibet – to the outside world.

This was when the media seized on a monk – the Dalai Lama – heads of State willingly met with. One fact would have been enough to draw attention to him: no one – not even the Communists – had considered replacing him.

In his memoirs the Dalai Lama relates in near-mathematical terms how a group of lamas set out in search of the reincarnation of the 14th Dalai Lama, inspired by a vision granted to the Regent, who directed them to the right region and then to the very house. Arriving at the house, they asked for hospitality, but without divulging their identity. The household's small son went straight to the head of the group – who was disguised as a servant – and demanded "his" rosary, which in fact had belonged to the late Dalai Lama. Many different objects were shown to him and he recognized without fail all those that had belonged to the religious leader.

Totally beyond the comprehension of Westerners, such stories reveal the highly distinctive character of Tibet's religion, as well as its many enigmas. Yet it remains quite compatible with today's world and gives further point to André Malraux's remark that "The 21st century will be spiritual or it will not be."

Lhasa: the Potala palace

This monastery is the former residence of the Dalai Lamas. It is the perfect symbol of Tibetan architecture, for it combines the notions of royal palace, temple and pagoda. It is 110 meters (360 ft) high and 360 meters (1200 ft) wide. The site was first occupied by Songsten Gampo in the 7th century, but the present building dates from the 17th century. Using the hillside as foundations, its austere exterior is in marked contrast with the rich gold and red decoration to be found inside, together with the countless paintings, statues and sacred fabrics – all intended as reminders that in Tibetan Buddhism all is symbol.

Overleaf
Lhasa: Jokhand

This is Tibet's oldest monastery, established by Songsten Gampo in 651, but extended up until the 17th century. The Tibetans are deeply attached to it, legend describing it as built on the site of an ancient underground lake propitious to divination.

Burma

The history of Burma – or Myanmar as it now officially called – is among the stormiest of all this part of South-East Asia: despite the omnipresence of Buddhism, a religion that is nothing if not pacific, Burma has always been marked by warlike tendencies – and a penchant for changing its capital.

The latest capital – Rangoon or Yangon – is home to the tallest pagoda in the world, the Shwe Dagon complex, whose main spire reaches a height of 100 meters (330 ft). It is surrounded, moreover, by dozens of other pagodas whose gold and silver exteriors give the site an almost unreal look.

In fact Shwe Dagon's current appearance dates only from the 19th century, but the site is a very ancient one in religious terms, going back to the 6th century BC. At that time, it is said, a pagoda was built to house a remarkable treasure: eight hairs of the Buddha, brought by Indian merchants.

Tradition has it that the site, like others in Burma, was chosen by Buddha himself. Interestingly, we find Buddha represented in a very specific way in Burma: standing and pointing out a sacred spot with his right hand. The building of Mandalay, for example, is believed to have been decided on in this way.

The country we now call Burma owes its name to the aggressiveness of a people, the Burmans, who established themselves there in the early 11th century. It had previously been home to the highly civilized Pyu, considered a Tibeto-Burman people, and the Mon, relatives of the Khmers. The Mon capital was at Thaton, in the Irrawaddy delta in Lower Burma.

The fall of the Pyu is attributed to the Thais, and the momentary weakening of the Mon to the arrival of the Burmans from the north. Prosperous landholdings sprang up along the Irrawaddy, with rice as a major crop and the first capital, Pagan, being founded in the 9th century.

Two centuries later chief Anawratha founded the first Burman dynasty and destroyed Thaton, feeling that the Mon were too friendly with the Khmers. He was also responsible for the first irrigation projects, an important factor in the country's development. Anawratha took the Tripitaka, the sacred Buddhist texts, from the Mon and placed them in shrines in Pagan, although we cannot be sure he found them at Thaton.

At the time of its decline in the 13th century, Pagan was home to 5000 religious and secular monuments, of which 1500 survive in the form of remains.

The earliest monuments in Pagan date from the 2nd century and to today's visitor the city seems an enormous hymn to Buddha, with countless stupas, pagodas and temples testifying to centuries of Buddhist presence. However the northern borders could not resist a fresh wave of invaders, the Mongols, who destroyed the power of Pagan and unleashed hundreds of years of internal quarrels: the Thais moved in and the province of Arakan and Pegu was taken from the Burmans.

Then came the rule of the Chan, relatives of the Mon, who established a new capital, Ava, of which no trace remains. The Mon preferred a port as their capital and as a result Pegu became the heart of a brilliant civilization. The Burmans retreated to Tungoo, where they regrouped their forces and conquered fresh territory. In 1539 the Burmans were once again masters of Burma and Pegu under King Tabinshweti, who expanded his kingdom as far as Ayutthaya before being assassinated by the Mon: once again Burma was torn by bloody conflict.

In the 17th century the capital was moved to Ava, the former Chan capital in the centre of the country.

In the 18th century Shwebo became the capital, followed by Ava (again) then Amarapura.

In 1859 the capital moved yet again, to Mandalay, set on a hill by the Irrawaddy. With Pagan and Shwe Dagon, Mandalay is one of the best reasons for taking the trouble to visit a country that does not encourage tourists: even though the Japanese destroyed the four square kilometers (1.5 square miles) of the palace – but not the walls – there remain a host of fascinating sites, not least the famous square pagoda of Kuthodaw.

The present capital was chosen by the English when they annexed a country they felt might cause problems with their Indian empire: their choice was the port city of Rangoon.

Rangoon: Shwe Dagon

Shwe Dagon is one of Buddhism's most sacred sites, an immense area of dozens of gleaming, overlapping secondary pagodas. Here we see the main pagoda, sheathed in gold and the tallest building in the Buddhist world. In his famous Geography, the early Greek historian Ptolemy makes reference to Burma as the Golden Chersonese, while Marco Polo speaks of the Kingdom of Mian.

Thailand: Ayutthaya

North of Bangkok, the oldest parts of the ruins of Ayutthaya, the former capital of Siam – as the country was called until 1939 – date from the mid-15th century. We owe the building of the capital to a certain Prince U-Thong, who was crowned king in 1347 under the name Ramadhibodhi; the city was the heart of the Kingdom of Ayutthaya, successor to the Kingdom of Sukhothai, founded in 1238. The Sukhothai period was a vital part of the country's history, as it led to a degree of unification, the introduction of writing and the spread of Theravada Buddhism.

U-Thong's unchallenged authority over his people was due to his status as a god-king at the head of a totally centralized state. His successors created all sorts of institutions, some of which were still functioning in the 19th century. Ayutthaya maintained its role as capital until 1767, the kingdom continuing to expand via bitter, ongoing battles with its near neighbors. Sukhothai was the first to fall; reduced to the status of vassal, its ruler Lu Thai became just another subject of the Siamese sovereign.

In 1431, the Khmers suffered the same fate, their armies being crushed in their own capital of Angkor. In 1767, however, the situation was reversed: armies from Burma swept through Ayutthaya, plundering the capital, destroying its treasures and massacring the people.

Overnight the fantastically wealthy capital was turned into ruins. Such was the extent of the destruction that the Chakri dynasty, based in Bangkok, abandoned the idea of rebuilding. The inhabitants who had managed to survive left the region and settled in the southern part of the kingdom of Siam.

Built on an island, the city of Ayutthaya occupied a highly strategic position near the confluence of no less than three rivers: the Mae Nam Pasak to the northeast; the Mae Nam Lop Buri to the northwest and the Chao Phraya, which ran around the city from west to south. Initially covering an area of five kilometers by three (10 square miles in all) the city was remarkably well planned for its time, with an elaborate grid of canals. The ruins cover this entire area, including nearby sections not actually on the island.

During Ayutthaya's four centuries of existence its thirty-three kings steadily made the city more and more beautiful, each adding – according to his beliefs and preferences – palaces, temples, pagodas or shrines adorned with stucco and dazzling gold.

With each new conquest the sovereigns assimilated fresh artistic concepts. The ruins of Ayutthaya reveal a subtle intermingling of very ancient Siamese traditions and notions borrowed

techniques of their own output. The most striking relic of the old city is Amida, the enormous bronze Buddha: the largest statue of its kind ever made in Thailand, it was housed in the Viharn Phra Mongkol Bopitr, an immense 15th-century shrine.

Despite its incredible size, no detail was overlooked and the shaping of the face reveals all the gentleness and benevolence that characterize the art of Ayutthaya.

Facing page
Nakhon Phanom:
the Phra That Phanom

Here on the Mekong in northeastern Thailand we are in an area whose rich history shows considerable Khmer influence. Situated in Wat Phanoni, this chedi is one of the country's most venerated places of pilgrimage.

from all over Asia, but especially from Sukhothai and the Khmer empire of Cambodia.

The city's heyday came in the 16th century, through a perfect combination of the arts, crafts and architecture.

Local work in lacquer, wood and bronze showed such a level of skill and refinement that many other kingdoms drew on Ayutthaya for the forms and

Many temples still stand among the ruins as testimony to the prosperity of a kingdom whose rulers were marked by a profound piety. The difficulty for the visitor is the sheer complexity and seeming disorder of a site on which countless prangs (towers forming part of local religious architecture), stupas (round reliquaries topped with a spire), chedis (buildings with the same function as stupas) and temples all rub shoulders.

Above
Chedis at Ayutthaya

At the heart of the artificial island formed by the confluence of the three rivers, Ayutthaya offers a striking group of ruined palaces and temples. The luxury of this Far Eastern capital impressed even the emissaries of Louis XIV. These chedis housed relics of Buddha and the saints.

Bangkok

Compared to those of other Eastern civilizations, the gleaming golden temples of Bangkok date from relatively recently. Historically speaking, the foundation of the city in the 18th century seems but a minor event.

Behind it lay the savage destruction of Ayutthaya by armies from Burma. As it happened a general named Phya Tak managed to escape; known for his earlier victories over the invaders, he succeeded in putting together a small army. With his men he went up the Chao Phraya river and settled in the village of Thon Buri, where he built a kind of parody of Ayutthaya; however, it was not long before his supporters, worried by his delusions of grandeur, replaced him with Phya Kari, the successor he himself had designated. Phya Kari had Phya Tak killed and himself crowned king, then crossed the river to found a new capital with a host of temples and palaces. Thus Bangkok was born, and with it the new king's dynasty. With the addition of the name of Rama, a Siamese hero, that same dynasty still rules today.

Following that of Sukhothai and Ayutthaya, the art of Bangkok is described as being in the Ratanakosin style. Begun in the late 18th century, the building of the city mostly took place in the 19th century. Time was short, given the number of temples, monasteries and palaces to be built, but one result of this was stylistic harmony for a style which had set out with the handicap of having to copy the past.

Architectural purists have often criticized the Ratanakosin style for its manneredness and ornamental exaggeration. Nonetheless we owe a debt of gratitude to those artists who pushed their imaginations to the limit in their efforts to honor Buddha via a remarkable use of colors and materials. The admirably maintained temples, for example, are marvelous oases of calm and greenery. Among those deserving of mention are Wat Po, Wat Phra Keo ("Temple of the Emerald Buddha"), Wat Mahathat, Wat Rachapradit, Wat Rajabopitr, Wat Suthat, Wat Somanat, Wat Benchamabopitr and many others, not to mention the Royal Palace and the National Museum, in the former palace of King Chulagonkorn.

Wat Phra Keo

One of the jewels of Thai architecture, this temple was built as the result of an accident. One day lightning struck a modest pagoda at Chiang Rai, but spared a number of objects including a stucco-covered Buddha. Soon, however, the stucco began to peel off, revealing a precious green Buddha made of jasper; such was the people's fervor that it became known as the Emerald Buddha. The statue was later transferred to Chiang Mai, where it was venerated – until it was stolen and taken to Vientiane by a young Laotian prince. When King Rama I conquered Laos, he brought the statue home and in the 18th century the Chakri dynasty built the Wat Phra Keo to house it.

Malaysia

Surrounded by Thailand, Indonesia and the Philippines, Malaysia is a special kind of entity in South-East Asia, covering two regions separated by the China Sea: the Malay Peninsula (excluding Singapore) at the southern tip of the Asian continent, and the states of Sabah and Sarawak on the island of Borneo.

Malaysia has long been a business and tourist crossroads for different peoples of both East and West, but has also found itself on the path of various invaders. As a result it has had no choice but to assimilate diverse and sometimes totally contradictory influences deriving from a long succession of occupiers.

An Indo-Malay civilization began to take shape as early as the second century AD, and went on to last no less than a thousand years. Permeated through and through with Buddhism and Hinduism, Malaysia adopted from the outset traditions, customs and rituals inherited from such great – and already extremely powerful – Asian kingdoms as Angkor (the Khmer empire in Cambodia) and, later, Ayutthaya in Thailand.

In the 8th century the country came under the control of the Khmers, whose rise remains one of the decisive political events in the history of South-East Asia. On the western coast of the Malay peninsula the archeological remains at Perak – among them the little temple built on the Sungei Batu Pahat floodplain – are eloquent testimony to the Khmer influence.

In 1400 the Javanese prince Parameswara set out to protect his capital, Temasek – now the city of Singapore – against the Siamese potentates of Ayutthaya. When he failed, the city was sacked and its people took refuge in Malacca, in southwestern Malaysia.

Selangor: the mosque of Sultan Salahuddin Abdul Aziz Shah

This splendid modern mosque is the jewel of the city of Shah Alam. Its dome is the largest in the world and each of its four minarets is over 100 meters (330 ft)

With the backing of the emperors of China, who were determined to put a stop to the Siamese occupation, this small village quickly became a flourishing centre for trade. Before his death Parameswara converted to Islam, thus introducing to Malaysia a religion that soon came to dominate the entire peninsula. Today Islam is still the official religion, but many others – among them Buddhism, Hinduism, Taoism and Christianity – are also recognized.

From the 16th century onwards the city of Malacca belonged successively to the Portuguese, the Dutch (well established in Java) and the English, who came to Penang in 1786.

The atmosphere and the petty intrigues of the English era are very well captured by Belgian writer Francis de Croisset in his 1936 novel Lady in Malacca.

Independent since 1957, the easygoing Malays have nonetheless kept certain habits from the colonial past, such as teaching English and driving on the left. In this tropical country the capital,

Kuala Lumpur has an unexpected look to it: sparkling skyscrapers rub shoulders with modern palaces and mosques in a setting of impeccable lawns and majestic palm trees.

Kuala Lumpur, however, is only one of Malaysia's many faces. This country of 330,000 square kilometers (128,000 square miles), comprising 13 states and 2 federal territories spread along a peninsula not far from the equator, offers the traveler incredible diversity.

Along the east and west coasts lie marvelous tropical beaches, while further inland rice paddies alternate with lakes and luxuriant forests. In the various state capitals gleaming mosques coexist peacefully with palaces, temples and the multicolored market stands, with their enchanting odors.

Modern Malaysia is a constitutional monarchy. The prime minister is head of the federal government and by tradition His Majesty the King is elected by the nation's leaders every five years.

**Perak:
the Ubudiah mosque**

Tin-mining brought wealth to the State of Perak, north of the State of Selangor, and it was here that Malaysia's first railroad was built. This mosque, with its splendidly maintained dome, is one of the oldest in the country.

Singapore

Situated at the southernmost point of the Malay Peninsula, the city of Singapore enjoys a privileged setting in the very heart of Asia.

Close to Thailand, the Philippines and Indonesia, and joined to Johore in Malaysia by a famous causeway over a kilometer (3300 ft) long, this republic comprises a main island and no fewer than 57 smaller islands. Its total area, on the other hand, is extremely small at only 623 square kilometers (243 square miles).

The earliest recorded historical references go back to the 14th century, when Singapore was still called Temasek, the "City of the Sea". In those early times this was, in fact, no more than a small village whose people lived by fishing. History moves on, however, and not long afterwards Temasek was taken over by the powerful Sri Vijaya empire. Legend has it that a Srivijayan prince once saw there an animal that looked to him like a lion: so he renamed the city Singa Pura, or "City of the Lion".

Today's Singapore is, in one respect at least, something of a 19th-century creation. The English dignitary Sir Stamford Raffles was looking for a headquarters for the British East India Company, dealing in spices and many other products. In 1819 he opted for Singapore: the city's strategic location and natural harbor seemed to him ideal for the establishing of a trading post.

So Singapore set about becoming a centre for international trade – between East and West – and has never looked back. At one point occupied by the Japanese for three years, it changed status a number of times before becoming an independent republic in 1965.

An interesting facet of life in Singapore is the way its 2.7 million people of different backgrounds – Chinese, Malay, Indian, Eurasian – live together without difficulty. Given this mix the government had no choice but to adopt four official languages – Mandarin, Tamil, Malay and English – while allowing each ethnic group to preserve its own cultural identity.

Side by side in Singapore the visitor sees mosques, churches, synagogues and Buddhist and Hindu temples – with impressive skyscrapers springing up among them.

Singapore

Without the problems of the Old and New Worlds, some South-East Asian countries are developing at an astonishing rate – and with a discretion matched only by their efficiency. Singapore enjoys a special status as the "Switzerland of the East", while remaining resolutely focused on the possibilities of the third millennium.

Indonesia

Sulawesi: Toraja country

Living in the centre of the island, between 1000 and 3000 meters (3300-10,000 ft) above sea level, the Toraja have retained a unique, highly structured social and religious system. The inhabitants are divided up into "free men" (10% of the population), two intermediate castes and the "slaves" who make up a good half of the total. The Dutch and later the Indonesian government attempted to free the slaves, but the latter refused: for fear of breaking a taboo by rebelling against the clan and the ancestors? Or for fear of losing a relatively comfortable social structure, with board and lodging guaranteed? In any case, for the Toraja it is not life on earth that counts, but what comes afterwards. The funeral of a Toraja nobleman drives this point home. Death is a three-phase affair, beginning with the clinical end of life, which is accorded no great importance: the eviscerated body remains in the house and continues to be offered symbolic nourishment. The official announcement of death comes only after the sacrifice of a buffalo, the pivotal animal of the Toraja culture. However the funeral ceremony, with its conferring of the status of ancestor, may not take place for twenty years: it involves bringing together the entire family and finding the money needed for the sacrifice of dozens of buffalo. A special village is built for the ceremony – which can last a month – and then destroyed. The dead man can then join the staring-eyed effigies of the ancestors in their cliffside tombs.

South of the Indian subcontinent lies Indonesia, a group of 13,777 more or less volcanic islands scattered across the Indian Ocean. Of this total, however, only 3000 are inhabited.

In the 19th century this vast archipelago, stretching from the Malay Peninsula to the Moluccas, still bore the mysterious, magical-sounding name of the Sunda Islands. For hundreds of years the region has been the subject of all sorts of Western fantasizing: islands covered with totally impenetrable jungle and inhabited by fantastic creatures; or exotic lands whose peoples – the Batak of Sumatra, for example, or the Toraja of Sulawesi – lead idyllically primitive lives.

The facts are perhaps more prosaic, but in the modern world more interesting: Indonesia is the world's largest Muslim country; and during the first thousand years AD some of its islands were home to flourishing Hindu and Buddhist civilizations.

At the same time – and despite the efforts of Christian missionaries, among them St Francis Xavier – the inhabitants of the Greater and Lesser Sunda Islands remain in many cases strongly marked by animist traditions as well.

Indonesia lies just by the equator: it begins with Sumatra, south of Malaysia on the other side of the Straits of Malacca. In terms of size the contrast with tiny Singapore, opposite the north coast of Sumatra, is hardly to be believed. Indonesia is one of the most scattered countries on the planet, running all the way from Thailand to Papua-New Guinea. Looking from east to west its main islands are Sumatra, Java, Bali, the Flores group, and West Timor and Irian – the western part of New Guinea. To the north are Borneo, Sulawesi (the former Celebes) and the Moluccas.

The largest single island is Borneo, with its 736,000 sq. kilometers (287,000 sq. miles), but the most densely populated is Java (132,000 sq. km/52,000 sq. miles) with around 100 million inhabitants. Java is home to the Borobudur temple complex, dating from the Sailendra dynasty, whose kings dominated the region over a thousand years ago. Yet it is minuscule Bali (5561 sq. km/2172 sq. miles) that has done the most to make Indonesia known throughout the world.

Cambodia

The Khmer empire succeeded in establishing itself in the region in the early 9th century, through the exceptionally forceful personalities of its kings. Having driven out the Javanese, they extended their landholdings from east to west and set up their capital at Angkor, in what is now Cambodia.

This choice reflected two vital necessities: they needed a capital situated at the very heart of their mighty empire; and such a capital had to have an ample supply of rivers and streams. At the height of their power, in the 11th century, the Khmers controlled an area comprising present-day Cambodia, Laos, southern Siam (Thailand) and the northern part of Malaysia.

For five hundred years Angkor was meticulously maintained and embellished, becoming in the process the very symbol of Khmer art with its subtle mix of local traditions, neighboring influences and personal input.

When, in the 19th century, the French explorer Henri Mouhot made his way into Angkor, the long-

abandoned city was so invaded by tropical vegetation that three quarters of its buildings could no longer be seen. Today the clearing process is complete and visitors can see the city as it was in the time of its greatest glory.

The jewel of this immense complex is Angkor Wat, built by Suryavarman II early in the 12th century. Dedicated to Vishnu, it also served as a tomb for its builder and, like the other main temples, was part of the cult of the deified ancestors and the deva raja or god-king.

Not far away, Jayavarman VII founded the city of Angkor Thom in the late 12th century. This represented, so to speak, a final spurt of energy before the beginning of the decline of the Khmer world.

True, the empire would live on for another two hundred years, but its power was gradually worn down by the Vietnamese and the Thais.

Built around the Bayon temple, the city was marked by the king's recent conversion to Buddhism, but even its striking beauty cannot conceal the first signs of decay.

Angkor Wat

The name means Temple-City. Dating from the 12th century, this is the largest sacred architectural complex known to man and has a place on the UNESCO World Heritage listing. The number and size of the buildings did not prevent the artists of the time from covering them with meticulously accurate images of everyday life.

China

The Homo Erectus remains found at Lantian allow us to date the settlement of China to 600,000 years ago. Later, traces of painted pottery from the Neolithic indicate a Middle-Eastern influence.

With their funerary and domestic furniture, and their chariots and bronze horses, the tombs of Zhengzhou and Anyang mark the emergence of Chinese civilization under the first dynasty: that of the Shang (1770-1050 BC). Religious inscriptions on bones and tortoise shells reveal the birth of Chinese writing. Iron and glass made their appearance in the 13th century BC, but the bronzes of the Zhou dynasty (1050-221 BC) are of cruder workmanship. In addition to their frequent battles, the courts of the Warring Kingdoms (481-221 BC) strove to outdo each other in terms of sheer luxury: bronze and jade items were richly ornamented with gold, silver, turquoise and malachite.

This was the era of a Chinese culture common to the various rival states. Philosophers, scholars and masters traveled from one royal court to another, craftsmen produced exquisite lacquerware and paintings on silk. To bar the way to the nomadic hordes, Qin Shih Huangti built the Great Wall of China. The dynasty founded by this first emperor (221-206 BC) was shortlived, but he left the world his name: Qin, pronounced "Chin", became "China". In his tomb near Xian was discovered an enormous buried army of 6400 soldier-statues.

Another tomb, that of Prince Liu Sheng at Mancheng, was found to contain 2800 burial objects made of gold, silver, jade, bronze and lacquer. His shroud and that of his spouse are made up of thousands of jade and gold plaques. The tomb was guarded by monumental statues of animals so realistic that they actually seem to be in movement. With the art of the Han dynasty (206 BC-220 AD) came the humanism of Confucius and mystical lyricism of the Taoists.

Chinese art and crafts made their way to Korea and, after the conquest of the silk route caravans in central Asia, to Vietnam. Gu Kaizhi is the earliest Chinese painter to have come down to us, in the form of a single, delicately harmonious work. The invasion of northern China by the barbarians brought down the Han dynasty, leading to the period of fragmentation of the Three Kingdoms and the Six Dynasties (220-581 AD). The caves at Dunhuang yielded 2500 sculptures and 45,000 square meters (almost half a million square feet) of wall paintings. At Yungang and Longmen the statues are cut into the rock. Buddhism became the state religion of the Wei kingdom in the north and the Greco-Buddhist style gradually evolved towards more Chinese forms in a host of sculptures and cave paintings.

The Great Canal and the state silos of Luoyang are the work of the Sui (581-618). Built on the classic checkerboard pattern, Chang'an belongs to the Tang dynasty (618-907). The new sculptures of Longmen mark the highpoint of an art combining realism and virtuosity. The Song dynasty (960-1279) is characterized by large-scale paintings made up of receding planes; this was the dynasty that restored unity after the divisions of the Five Dynasties (907-960). Self-taught, Guo Xi was the painter of the mystical Taoist journey, seeking to go to the heart of nature and forget the physical world. Emperor Huizong (1101-1126) was himself a painter and scholar.

The horses painted by Zhao Mengfu are typical of the Mongol dynasty of the Yuan (1280-1368), founded by Kubla Khan, grandson of Genghis Khan and host to Marco Polo.

Peking became the capital under the Ming (1368-1644), marking the return to a Chinese dynasty. Yongle built the Forbidden City, the Summer Palace and the Altar of Heaven, which have been restored several times. A number of pavilions and the monastery of Wu Dang Zhao are in the Tibetan lamaist style, this being the religion of the Qing (1644-1911), the Manchu invaders who were China's last dynasty. This whole period was one of decline.

The 20th century belonged to painting. Huang Binhong is a traditionalist, Pu Xinyu paints landscapes, Qi Baishi specializes in gardens, Fu Baishi developed a new conception of space. Xu Beihong was the first to use oils and Western techniques. Zao Wuqi moved to Paris, where he set about creating a synthesis of traditional Chinese painting, Impressionism and Picasso.

The Luoyang Buddhas

Discovered inside the caves at Luoyang, these gigantic Buddhas are reminiscent of those in Afghanistan, mutilated by the hordes of Genghis Khan and dynamited some years ago by the Talebans. Fortunately the Chinese authorities have protected the heritage left by previous civilizations and dynasties. Despite its enormous size, this face seems to radiate all the serenity Buddha invites us to share.

Korea

At the far eastern edge of Asia, Korea is a small peninsula ringed by the continent's greatest powers – a difficult situation for South Korea, whose area is only 99,200 sq. kilometers (38,750 sq. miles). If North Korea is included, the total is 221,500 sq. kilometers (86,500 sq. miles).

The first politically organized kingdom in Korea goes back to the third millennium BC. Its legendary founder Tan'gun named it Ko-Choson and established his capital at Pyongyang. The hundreds of years that followed saw a proliferation of independent kingdoms, but by the first century BC only the largest had managed to survive: Koguryo, Paekche and Silla.

The most powerful, Koguryo accounted for two thirds of Korea and part of Manchuria. Paekche, near Seoul, moved southwest to escape its dominance, but still made an enormous contribution to knowledge and culture in Japan.

Silla, the most recent, was in the southeast of the peninsula, with its capital at Kyongju. Ultimately it surpassed the other two and in 668 AD succeeded in unifying Korea and giving rise to a very distinctive civilization. Kyongju remains living testimony to the highly developed culture of Silla. However, a revolt led by a certain Kungye, from the north, rapidly gained ground in the south. One of Kungye's lieutenants, Wanggon, founded the kingdom of Koryo, which gave the country its name.

Profoundly Buddhist, the Koryo dynasty built temples, pagodas and shrines everywhere; more importantly still, it published the Tripitaka Koreana, one of the most comprehensive collections of Buddhist scriptures.

Late in the 14th century decline set in and power shifted to the kingdom of Chosun, founded by Li Songkye; Chosun's capital Hanyang stood on the site of what is now Seoul. Weary of what they saw as Buddhist privileges, the Hanyang sovereigns made Confucianism the state doctrine.

Despite its age-old links with China, Korea retained its individuality. However, frequent invasions caused enormous destruction and suffering, and late in the 16th century the country opted for an isolationist policy. Even in the 19th century, when Japan and China began opening up to the West, the "Country of Morning Calm" was still the "Hermit Kingdom" and practically unknown to the outside world.

Nonsan: Kwanch'oksa

Unjin Miruk (the "Buddha of the Future") is a thousand years old. At 18 meters (60 ft) this is Korea's tallest stone Buddha, but is only half as tall as the bronze Buddha in the Songnisan National Park. The statue is the focal point of this shrine, with everything about it suggesting Buddhist spirituality: the strange headpiece that resembles a pagoda, the long-lobed ears and the distinctive positioning of the hands.

At the end of the 19th century the peninsula became the scene of battles between foreign powers and in 1910 Korea was annexed by Japan.

At the end of the Second World War the defeat of Japan meant independence for Korea, but other, purely political problems now divided the people into democrats in the south and Communists in the north. The bloody conflict that resulted – the Korean War – concluded with the signing of an armistice in 1953, but the split has never healed.

Japan

The kingdom of Yamato, in the Nara region, emerged out of a grouping of clans in the 6th century, at the same time as Buddhism was coming to Japan from China via Korea. By this time the Japanese had already adopted Chinese writing and other aspects of Chinese culture.

The 12th century brought war between the Taira and Minamoto clans; the latter emerged victorious and created the institution of the shogun, the hereditary commander in chief. Now no more than a figurehead, the emperor moved to Kyoto. Fighting continued between the central authority – the shogun – and local lords, and one result was the building of the Himeji fortress.

Today Himeji is an industrial city of 500,000 people, situated not far from Japan's Inland Sea. Its castle (jo) is the most famous and the most beautiful in the entire country: for some its silhouette is reminiscent of an egret, such a frequent sight on the rice fields of the plain, while others see in it the shape of a heron about to take flight. The site was a strategic one, as Himeji controlled access to the western provinces.

The feudal lords, or daimyo, rose against the shogun, but continued to indulge in bloody, pointless fighting between clans. In 1,346A first fortress was built by Akamatsu Sadanori on the hill of Himeyama.

A general named Toyotomi Hideyoshi took control of the fort in 1577. Of peasant origin, he had succeeded in conquering the western provinces, becoming shogun and reuniting Japan by sheer armed force. Toyotomi enlarged Himeji castle, built a three-story fortified keep and lived there for several years.

In 1601, Ikeda Terumasa, the son-in-law of Tokugawa Leyasu, rebuilt the castle from the ground up: this is the fortress so admired today, with its five-story keep and its three smaller towers. The building process took eight years.

Tokugawa Leyasu was Toyotomi's lieutenant. In 1600 he had crushed the last revolt of the great feudal lords, going on to found a veritable dynasty of shoguns that held the real power in Japan from 1600 to 1868. During that period the official imperial dynasty had to settle for a purely symbolic role. Tokugawa Leyasu brought the lords to heel, forcing them to spend half the year in Edo – the old name for Tokyo – while the emperor remained in Kyoto. Considered as traitors, the country's 600,000 Christians were hunted down and persecuted. Over six centuries Himeji-jo was host to thirteen families and forty-eight lords. The country was at peace and the castle built in 1601 never had to face a siege; its only enemy was the ravages of time, but it was thoroughly restored in 1963.

Officially declared a "National Treasure", the castle had been designed as an invulnerable fortress and a clear demonstration of the central government's power and prestige. It rises on an impressive foundation of cut stone and its keep overlooks a complex of moats, walls, doors and courtyards intended to frustrate the most determined attack. The walls included rectangular loopholes for the archers, while the defenders with guns had the choice of round, square or triangular ones. Other openings allowed those inside to welcome the enemy with stones and boiling water.

The lord's main palace or honmaru was at the foot of the keep in the first courtyard; his family lived in a palace in the second courtyard and his vassals and servants in the third. The other courtyards contained stores for arms, food and munitions. Life for the lords was peaceful and sophisticated. The keep itself was not lived in. It was intended as a last line of defense for the lord – and eventually for his ritual suicide (seppuku) should he decide not to surrender.

From the fifth floor the visitor has a great view: the castle and its defenses, the moats, the grounds, the modern city, the surrounding countryside and, further away, the Inland Sea, the Ieshima islands and the mountain ranges to the north.

Ideally the castle needs to be seen by night as well as by day; that way you can get some idea of what life must have been like at the time of Japan's feudal wars. And why not back up your impressions with some of the films of Akira Kurosawa, that unrivaled chronicler of the period: The Seven Samurai (1954) for example or, more recently, Kagemusha (1980) and Ran (1985).

Himeji-jo

Often called the "Castle of the White Heron", Himeji-jo was the high point of one of the art forms of the Empire of the Rising Sun: the shogun fortress. To prove their invincibility, the builders of Himeji-jo set out to create something completely new by situating their castle in an open space. From the central keep, 50 meters (165 ft) high, they had a perfect view of the entire region. On a clear day you can see all the way to the Inland Sea and its many islands.

New York

Manhattan before 9/11

This gleaming, metallic vision of New York belongs to the past, but it looks as though the new Manhattan will be even more impressive. The destruction of the Twin Towers dealt a terrible blow to the surrounding buildings, some of which also had to be demolished. New York covers an area of 800 square kilometers (300 square miles) and is divided into five boroughs: Manhattan, the Bronx, Brooklyn, Queens and Staten Island. Manhattan, the "heavenly country" of the local Indians, is the city's hub, covering 60 sq. kilometers (23 sq. miles). The best way to discover New York is to go to the 102nd floor of the Empire State Building (380 meters/1250 ft high) at the corner of Fifth Avenue and 34th Street. To the north you see the Rockefeller Center, the "Gothic" cathedral of St Patrick, patron saint of the city's large Irish community, and the 300 hectares (720 acres) of Central Park. Beyond lies Harlem. Westwards you look down on the Hudson River, New Jersey and Staten Island. To the south are the skyscrapers of Wall St, focus of attention of banks all over the world. The Hudson is elegantly spanned by the Brooklyn, Manhattan and Verrazano bridges, while out in the middle of Hudson Bay the Statue of Liberty, designed by the Frenchman Bartholdi, "lights up the world". Eastwards lie the East River, the United Nations building, Queens and Brooklyn. Fifth Avenue is typically Manhattan, but so too are the lights on Broadway, the artists in Greenwich Village, the ideograms in Chinatown and the special features of a host of different neighborhoods.

Rising like a surrealistic forest of steel and glass, the skyscrapers of Manhattan tend to make us forget how New York began: as a port. Now the world's third busiest, this port that has since welcomed countless thousands of immigrants. And since 1886 the immense Statue of Liberty has been there to greet visitors.

The first European to set foot here was the Florentine explorer Verrazano, in 1524. Sailing under the colors of François I, King of France, he named the spot New Angoulême: François' father had been Count of Angoulême.

Preoccupied with his conflicts with Charles V of Spain, the king paid little heed to this discovery and Verrazano continued southwards, only to be eaten by cannibals in the West Indies. Almost a century later the English mariner Henry Hudson, employed by the Dutch, arrived and bought the island of Manhattan from an Algonquin Indian – even though it was actually lived on by the Iroquois.

The name then became New Amsterdam – until the English seized it in 1664 and renamed it New York. Reclaiming it in 1673, the Dutch called it New Orange, but the following year the English took back "their" land. Thus New York became English-speaking, but its administrators granted trade rights to the Dutch, who had already proved themselves in both Europe and Asia. Things moved fast in the "New World", with immigrants of every nationality and creed arriving every day, in flight from poverty and religious persecution. Freedom of belief was officially declared in 1707 and Independence in 1783. Slavery was abolished in 1827.

With Europe plunged into the troubled times of the French Revolution and the Napoleonic Empire, the people of New York set about making a success of things. By 1860 the city already had 800,000 inhabitants and was North America's leading business centre.

Despite the terrorist attacks of 11 September 2001, its people still have the same enthusiasm as their ancestors and the city is still the nerve centre for the economy, finance and the arts. At street level those impossibly tall buildings can seem extremely hostile, but the openminded visitor will find an unexpectedly warm, colorful atmosphere.

Dakota

Mount Rushmore is universally known for its giant sculptures, cut directly into the wall of granite and representing the faces of four famous presidents: George Washington, Thomas Jefferson, Abraham Lincoln and Theodore Roosevelt.

This near-surrealistic setting was the location for one of Alfred Hitchcock's most spectacular and best-known films, North by Northwest, starring Cary Grant, Eva Marie Saint and James Mason.

Situated 40 km (25 miles) southwest of Rapid City in the Black Hill region of South Dakota, the Mount Rushmore National Memorial is both an enormous tourist success and an extraordinary technical feat. Begun in 1927 by the sculptor Gutzon Borglum, who was then sixty years old, the presidential faces rise to a height of 18 meters (60 ft).

George Washington, first president of the United States, is principally known for his fight for Independence. Born into a family of modest means in Virginia in 1732, he was interested in three things: the land he owned, his family and politics. In 1774 he represented Virginia in the first Congress of the thirteen colonies and the following year saw him made commander in chief of the army.

The War of Independence against the British was not slow in coming and on 4 July 1776 Independence was declared, each colony becoming a state with its own Constitution. Washington resigned from the army and was elected President of the United States, first in 1789 and again in 1792. He refused to stand for a third term and died in 1799.

Thomas Jefferson (1743-1826) was also born in Virginia, but into a well-off family. He became a lawyer at the age of twenty-four. In 1775 he took part in the writing of the Declaration of Independence and was elected governor of Virginia in 1779. With James Madison he founded the Democratic-Republican party. He was elected Vice-President in 1796 and President from 1801 to 1809. A liberal thinker and a reader of Jean-Jacques Rousseau, he based his political program on four points: power for the states, rejection of the idea of a central bank, a predominant role for agriculture, and the example given by the French Revolution.

In 1803 he bought Louisiana from Napoleon Bonaparte for a ridiculously small sum and in doing so doubled the area of the United States as they then existed. The "Louisiana Purchase" was the beginning of the great move westwards.

He spent his later years on his estate at Monticello, in Virginia. The many letters that have come down to us reveal a politician whose ideas were as generous as they were complex. The Jefferson era marked the beginning of American bipartisan politics as we now know it.

Abraham Lincoln (1809-65) was a native of Kentucky who had practiced a variety of professions as he worked his way through law school. He entered politics in 1834, was elected to Congress in 1846 and became a member of the new Republican Party when it was founded in 1854. In November 1860 he won the presidential election.

A month later the Civil War broke out, lasting until 1865. In spite of the decision taken by Congress, eleven Southern states were determined to retain the system of slavery; they decided to secede from the Union, but Lincoln's "Federal" troops ultimately defeated the Southern "Confederates".

Abraham Lincoln was shot dead on 14 April 1865 by John Wilkes Booth, a mentally deranged actor who took him by surprise in his box at a theatre in Washington.

Scion of a wealthy New York family, Theodore Roosevelt (1858-1919) studied law at Harvard. A passionate student of history, he was a Republican congressman from 1882 to 1884, before settling on his ranch in Dakota. Roosevelt was a man of action: chief of police in New York in 1895, then assistant secretary for the navy, he led the war against Spain in Cuba in 1898. He went on to become Governor of New York, before being elected President of the United States in 1901 and again in 1904.

As a politician, Roosevelt was wily and ambitious. When divisions within the Republican Party led to its breakup in 1912, he formed the Progressive Party. But the presidential election was carried off by the Democrat Woodrow Wilson.

Mount Rushmore

Since its completion in 1942, millions of visitors have come to contemplate the 18-meter (60 ft) faces of Washington, Jefferson, Lincoln and Roosevelt sculpted into the granite cliff-face. This colossal tribute to those considered the nation's four greatest presidents is typical of a time when the New World readily combined economic success and a taste for the grandiose

Utah

"Red rocks standing upright like men, in a basin-shaped canyon": this was the Paiute Indians' description of Bryce Canyon, where they found life far from easy.

The canyon was named after a Mormon pioneer, Ebenezer Bryce. After living there for five years he described it as "a hell of a place to lose a cow".

The atmosphere in the canyon is so strange that it is very easy to start thinking in terms of "another world": you find your eyes scanning the rock walls in search of the traces of those long-lost dinosaurs.

And then there are the incredible colors: an endlessly shifting range of pinks, reds, and elusive blues. In the space of just a few minutes or a few yards the astonished visitor sees pink change to purple and then, just as quickly, the purple to blue.

But Bryce Canyon has other things to offer in addition to its magnificent landscapes, being rich in animal life as well: the commonest mammals are the mule deer, but there are also squirrels, coyotes, pumas, porcupines, woodchucks, prairie dogs and all sorts of other creatures.

Between May and October the canyon is home to 164 species of nesting birds, among them bluejays, swallows, swifts, woodpeckers and robin redbreasts. Many of the animals migrate elsewhere in October, the mule deer, pumas and coyotes, for example, seeking warmer conditions at a lower altitude.

Almost all the birds leave, the exceptions being the jays, crows, owls and falcons, who seem to like it there all year round. Hunting has reduced animal numbers and some species – grizzlies, wolves and others – are no longer to be found there. The elk, puma and black bear have become extremely rare.

The ruggedness of the landscape is decisive in terms of flora. The sides are too steep for anything to take root, but plant life is far from absent: the canyon floor is home to juniper, stone pine, spruce, birch and fir, especially towards Rainbow Point and Yovimpa Point. The nature and extent of the forest is very variable, according to altitude and rainfall. Springtime and early summer are the best times for wildflower lovers: irises, asters, clematis, primroses and a host of other colorful, highly perfumed species.

Bryce Canyon

This isn't just any old canyon: the fantastic landscape you see here is part of a gigantic amphitheatre cut into the Pink Cliffs. And Pink Cliffs is part of a series of slopes called the Grand Staircase – in fact it is the highest point of the staircase, and is made up of sedimentary rock whose yellow and pink tints stem from the presence of iron oxide; the purples and blues are caused by manganese. The sedimentary rock settled at the bottom of the enormous lakes that covered this region some 50 or 60 million years ago. A geological uplift began 13 million years ago, finally pushing up to a height of 3000 meters (10,000 ft) before being attacked by erosion. Interestingly, wind has played no part in creating these sculpted forms, which are entirely the work of water. The fantastic shapes make you think of all sorts of things: fairy castles in some cases, or soldiers marching off towards some dream of glory.

Mexico

Deep in Central America, the civilization of the Mayas achieved its high point in the 9th century AD. It comprised villages and cities of different sizes, whose inhabitants were quick to achieve a reputation for bravery and for their intellectual and artistic abilities. One major puzzle remains: why, at the dawn of the second millennium AD, did the Mayas suddenly abandon their villages and highly developed cities? One theory is that this desertion was the result of social upheavals or peasant revolts in which the underclasses exterminated their military, political and religious leaders.

Serpent" in the Mayan language – also known in Spanish as El Castillo, the castle. At its top is a tall, perfectly preserved temple. Four staircases of 91 steps lead to the top: 364 steps in all. When we add the step at the entry to the temple, the total is 365 – the number of days in a year.

Chichen Itza is also home to the largest known Toltec pelota court: 166 x 68.5 meters (550 x 225 ft). Here too we find the Temple of the Tigers and the Temple of the Warriors, the latter built over an earlier place of worship dedicated to Chaac Mool, god of rain and corn.

Facing page
Chichen Itza: the "Church"

At some distance from the "Castle" and the Temple of the Warriors, in the group of buildings known as the "Nuns' Convent", stands the small "Church". This is a typical example of the art of Puuc, in northern Yucatan, and is older than the other Toltec and Mayan buildings. The facade is generously ornamented with masks of the god Chaac.

Whatever the case, the Mayan empire fell into decay. But the political vacuum did not last long, as the Toltecs, a people from the region of Tula, took over the now independent provinces of Yucatan. They imposed the leadership of the god-king Quetzalcoatl, the "Feathered Serpent", and set up their capital at Chichen Itza in the jungle of northern Yucatan.

Neither totally Mayan nor totally Toltec, this splendid archeological site remains the most fascinating example so far discovered of work done by Mayans following ideas and plans that betray the Toltec way of thinking. On the northern part of the site rises the stepped pyramid of Kukulkan – "Feathered

Passionately interested in astronomy, the Toltecs had an observatory in each of their cities. In Chichen Itza this building, known in Spanish as El Caracol, the Snail – its spiral staircase resembles a snail's shell – is a round tower, rising above the luxuriant vegetation to provide a clear view of the heavens. This enabled the Toltec astronomers to establish with perfect accuracy the length of the solar year: 365 and one-quarter days. At the beginning of the 13th century the Toltecs were supplanted by the Aztecs, who also established themselves in Chichen Itza. But the major disruption was to come with the arrival of the Spanish conquistadors.

Above
The Temple of the Warriors and the "Thousand Columns"

Set at the end of the great ceremonial esplanade of Chichen Itza, this temple was even more awe-inspiring in the past. It was twice as high and the columns supported a roof that made the entry truly monumental. Many people consider this the ultimate masterpiece of pre-Columbian architecture.

Guatemala

At the height of their power the Mayas occupied an enormous area of Central America. Archeologists estimate that in all this civilization extended over some 325 square kilometers (126,000 square miles).

However, it seems that between 1500 BC – when the Mayan empire began to take shape – and the conquest of the New World by Cortes in the 16th century, the urban centers moved from the south towards the north. Around the year 1000 BC groups of people and their governments moved into the southern part of the empire, an area including northern Guatemala and southern Mexico.

Towards the 8th century BC this early civilization began to weaken and its leaders decided on a move north, towards Yucatan: here temples like those of Labna, Souyil and Uxmal are eloquent testimony to the grandeur of the Mayas.

The Toltec invasion put paid to the classical Maya era, but the new arrivals quickly showed themselves the equals of their predecessors, witness the fabulous archeological site of Chichen Itza.

The ancient city of Tikal in northern Guatemala is the oldest Mayan ruin so far discovered. It is also the largest, with over 3000 separate buildings spread over 10 square kilometers (6 square miles).

Discovered in 1877 by the Swiss explorer Gustav Bernouilli, deep in the heart of the virgin forest, the ruins of Tikal have long been lovingly cared for by archeologists from the University of Pennsylvania.

The site is marked out by three distinct acropolises: on the central – and largest – one stands an enormous five-story palace, the only one of its kind in the entire Mayan empire.

What is striking here is not so much the quality of the building as the sheer scale. The "Cresterias", as these pyramid-temples are called in Spanish, are the highest buildings in all pre-Columbian America. Up to 70 meters (230 ft) tall, they rise impressively above the surrounding forest. Interestingly, archeologists have established that these elaborately decorated accumulations of stone had no political or religious purpose: this is an example of art for art's sake, of artists giving free rein to their imagination.

Tikal

All over the site are standing stones, all sculpted along the same lines: a human figure seen in profile and surrounded by hieroglyphs. This form of writing is still little understood: two thirds of its "alphabet" has yet to be deciphered. However experts have succeeded in reading the dates and the names of gods cut into the stone. The oldest, the Red Stone of Tikal, dates from 292 AD and probably marks the first occupation of the site. However the experts also agree that the actual construction and ongoing extension of the city date from the 5th and 6th centuries.

Columbia: the Bogotá Gold Museum

Founded in 1939, the magnificent Gold Museum in Bogotá is home to a collection – unique in the world – of tens of thousands of examples of jewelry, finery and objects made of gold and precious stones.

These works of art represent several pre-Columbian civilizations, the best-known being those of the Chibcha (or Muisca) and Quimbaya Indians. Long established in the region, these peoples saw their political and social structures wiped out by the Spanish conquest in the 16th century.

In their greed the conquistadors plundered the temples, massacred all the Indians who dared to put up any resistance and loaded their ships with the treasures of the Andes, taking them away to Spain. They believed they had found the legendary kingdom of El Dorado ("the gilded one").

This long-dreamed place of abundance and wealth had its origins in a Muisca custom. A naked man, his body coated with grease and powdered gold, plunged into the sacred waters of the crater lake of Guatavita. When he emerged, gleaming in the rays of the supreme sun god Bochica, he was taken onto a raft bearing all the highest dignitaries.

The raft then moved to the centre of the lake, where handfuls of gold and emeralds were thrown into the water as an offering to the gods. Along the shoreline, the faithful chanted prayers.

It was this ritual, portrayed on the Museum's famous golden raft, that so excited the covetousness of the conquistadors.

The gold and emerald mines had been worked by the pre-Columbian Indians since the 7th century BC. The Indians were highly skilled goldsmiths and their art was mainly religious.

The temples were decorated with precious stones and covered with a fine layer of gold. In their rituals, ceremonies and sacrifices to the gods they used partly human figures and votive statuettes. They wore gold jewelry in the course of their everyday lives and it was buried with them when they died.

The pre-Columbian peoples also created such alloys as tumbaga, made up of gold, copper and silver in varying proportions. Producing a chemical reaction by adding the sap of a special plant, they created a substance resembling pure gold. Thus it was that the Spanish invaders were gulled more than once, blinded as they were by what seemed an incredible display of riches.

The peaceful Quimbaya people lived in the area around the river Cauca and were remarkable goldsmiths. All that remains of them now is their sumptuous output: finely worked jewelry – rings, earrings, nose ornaments ("narigueras"), pendants, diadems – and splendid helmets, breastplates, gold masks, ceremonial statuettes and other treasures.

On them they carved realistic images of eagles, owls and frogs, creatures they regarded as sacred.

The Chibchas, also known as the Muiscas, lived in the upland valleys east of the river Magdalena, with one of their most powerful tribes at Tunja. Their customs are known to us in more detail: their skills included farming, weaving, ceramics and goldsmithing.

Less gifted as goldsmiths than the Quimbaya, they nonetheless produced magnificent coins. They too used the tumbaga technique for making jewels and religious statues.

Their many deities included the goddess Bachue, creator of the world and the Chibcha people.

The Sun and Moon were also venerated as gods and a number of Chibcha myths have come down to us via oral tradition. We know that certain animals – the frog was the symbol of the Chibcha nation – and certain stones, considered as representing the ancestors, were held sacred.

The ceremonies held on Lake Guatavita were incredibly spectacular. The raft symbolizing the legend of El Dorado is now in the Gold Museum. Other legends tell of the origins of the human race or of episodes in the life of certain caciques or chieftains.

Other tribes – the Sinu, Tolima, Calima and Tairona – were also goldsmiths, although the levels of skill and artistic achievement varied considerably.

Their origins, however, remain a mystery and we still do not know how long these peoples had been living in "New Grenada", as the conquistadors named Colombia.

A Tolima breastplate

The El Dorado raft and this geometrical breastplate are the stars of the show at the Bogotá Gold Museum. Gold had no monetary value for the Indians, but as a symbols of eternity it was a fundamental part of a civilization ever in search of ways of communicating with the gods. The Indians of this region had their breastplates buried with them, which led the conquistadors to plunder their graves.

San Agustin

Situated in the southern part of Colombia, San Agustin is the oldest and largest archeological remnant of a still little-known civilization spread over a vast and very fertile part of the Andes.

Statues, shrines, chambers and relief-sculpted stones cover the site, yet no one has ever been able to establish the origin or the identity of the people responsible for its creation.

Some experts see certain Peruvian and Bolivian civilizations, notably that of Tahuanaco, a few miles from Lake Titicaca, as direct descendants of the San Agustin people and culture. Unfortunately this point of view remains purely theoretical, as there is no clear evidence for or against it.

One thing seems certain, however: this was a very ancient civilization. When the conquistadors arrived in the 16th century the site, completely swallowed up by the virgin forest, had already been abandoned for several centuries.

Victims of the pitiless influence of the Inquisition, the Spanish invaders were shocked by these stone idols, some of which displayed an erect phallus, and in the name of Christ they set about systematically destroying the precious vestiges of an isolated, totally unknown civilization. Two centuries late the site underwent further depredations at the hands of gold prospectors.

San Agustin was finally granted officially protected status in the early 20th century. It seems probable that the local civilization met its end towards the end of the 8th century AD, but archeologists still cannot reach agreement on its origins. The most striking remains to be found on the site are the enormous, monolithic statues: almost all of them are different and the largest are 4 meters (13 feet) tall.

The most elaborate examples doubtless represent gods: as a rule four fangs emerge from an over-large mouth, while two enormous eyes flank a nose with dilated nostrils. The hands are placed on the chest, often brandishing various objects: scepters, tools, trophies and other things. Some of them still bear traces of the multicolored paint that must initially have covered them.

San Agustin

Over an area of 500 square kilometers archeologists have discovered 450 statues, but they believe that there were once thousands of them. Each one is different and has a marked symbolic and social significance. The symbolism lies in the use of the many faces of the Indian pantheon: ibis, lizard, snake, frog and so on. The social significance is expressed in the nature of the different groups portrayed: the clergy or the army, craftsmen, etc. Despite – or because of? – its pagan character, the Spaniards named the site after St Augustine.

These statues are thought to be individual funerary monuments designed to confer immortality on the dead. In addition to the statues, archeologists have discovered underground shrines containing sarcophagi

over 2 meters (6.5 ft) long and burial items from which no real conclusions can be drawn. In an attempt to throw light on the mystery, experts in Andean civilizations are trying to draw parallels between San Agustín and two other sites not far away: the Cauca Valley and the region around Tierradentro. Both present surprising resemblances to the great monoliths and sanctuaries of San Agustín.

Peru

High in the Andes, at 2430 meters (8000 ft) above sea level, is one of the most fascinating of all the Inca fortresses in Peru: Machu Picchu.

Around the year 1200 a small, warlike group burst onto the Peruvian high plains: these were the Incas, and they set up their capital at Cuzco. Lavish buildings still testify to the splendor of this civilization, which created extraordinary palatial complexes throughout its empire.

It was not until the reign of Pachacuti, in 1428, that the Incas decided to undertake a campaign of far-reaching territorial conquest. After subjugating all the independent local tribes, they set about conquering the powerful empires existing in Peru at the time.

The Chimus, for example, were unchallenged masters of the entire northern part of the country, but they put up little resistance and the Incas found themselves in control of a territory extending from the equator to Chile. When the Spanish conquistadors seized Peru in 1532, the Inca empire, firmly established for over a century, seemed at the height of its glory and power.

Better than any other architectural example, Machu Picchu symbolizes the special genius of the Incas. North of Cuzco, in a depression formed by the river Urubamba and overlooking its turbulent waters, the city stands on a ridge flanked by two rocky peaks: Machu Picchu, the "old mountain"(3140 meters / 10,360 ft) and Huayna Picchu, the "young mountain" (2743 meters / 9050 ft).

We find a number of vague mentions of the city in accounts by 19th century travelers, but the real discovery of Machu Picchu – abandoned and forgotten for four hundred years – was the work of the North American archeologist Hiram Bingham, who in 1911 and pretty much by pure chance, found his way into the Inca fortress.

Begun during the reign of Pachacuti – or perhaps of his successor – the city of Machu Picchu seems never to have been completed. Partially cut stones left lying about with no attempt at organization prove that the city had been hastily abandoned by the Incas who were still building it.

Machu Picchu

At the centre of the fortress is the "Torreon", cut into the rock probably as a place for sacrifices to the sun god Inti, the supreme Inca divinity. The religion of the Inca people was based on the firm conviction that the true Inca is a direct descendant of the sun. The Torreon is complemented by an elaborately equipped cave; according to Hiram Bingham this is a royal tomb, doubtless intended to receive a mummified body. However this and other notions must remain pure hypotheses, given the total absence of inscriptions and ornamentation at Machu Picchu. Cutting through the Torreon complex is a series of sixteen pools cut into the rock, the water cascading down from one to another. We still do not know if they served a religious or purely utilitarian purpose, such as irrigation or water supply for the settlement. Towards the east is the residential section, with its houses, baths and aqueducts; the religious buildings are to the west. On a high rocky spur stands the "intihualimi", the "place where the sun is imprisoned". This is a kind of sundial intended to function as a calendar.

Chile

Set in the Pacific Ocean 3700 kilometers (2300 miles) from the coast of Chile and 4050 kilometers (2500 miles) from Tahiti, Easter Island is no more than a tiny volcanic outcrop – yet for its inhabitants this was "the navel of the world". Its hundreds of colossal statues or moais, sculpted in volcanic rock from the Rano-Raraku volcano and weighing several tons each, turn their backs to the ocean as steadfastly as they keep the secret of their mysterious origin. Standing from three to six meters (10-20 ft) high, they are topped with a cap or chignon of red stone that adds two meters (6.5 ft) to their height. Just what civilization does their presence bear witness to? And how were they transported – for ten and sometimes twenty kilometers (6-12 miles)?

Fantastic giants with enormous, staring eyes of white coral: some of them have fallen, others remain unfinished. Gods, probably, erected somewhere between 1000 and 1500 AD on "ahu", stone altars created by the individual clans for whom each moai was the image of an ancestor. Numerous stone carvings show the figure of the bird-man and Maké-Maké, the mythological creator of mankind. There are, too, the rongo-rongo, enigmatically carved stone tablets bearing mute witness to some vanished religion.

As part of the cult of the bird-man, or Tangata Manu, ceremonies were held each year at Orongo. In a grueling physical ordeal, he who brought back the first tern's egg was proclaimed military chief and

Easter Island: Anakena beach

At its highest point, this volcanic island is 560 meters (1850 ft) above sea level. Here we see its only real sandy beach: legend has it that this was the landing-place of the first king, Hotu Matua, when he arrived from Tahiti.

second king for a year. The ceremonies organized by the priests also involved human sacrifices.

There were ten clans, all governed by the same king. The first king came to the northern part of the island accompanied by his wife Vakai a Hiva, numerous servants and several hundred subjects. His successors up until 1862 comprised some thirty sovereigns, all from the same Miru clan. The clans had a strict hierarchy: priests (chosen from among the nobility), warriors, farmers and slaves.

Tradition tells of inter-clan conflicts, triggered perhaps by overpopulation, and also of an invasion that saw the "Long Ears" doing battle with the "Short Ears". These battles could explain the partial destruction of certain statues.

Another tradition accounts for the abandoning of the 300 unfinished statues by the terrifying passage of a comet.

It would seem that Easter Island was first inhabited in the 5th century AD. But where did those inhabitants come from? Some experts have traced them back to Peru, although the majority are in favor of Polynesia. One thing for certain, though: the island was discovered by Europeans, in the form of the Dutch navigator Roggeveen, on Easter Sunday 1722. Its population was partly massacred in raids by Peruvian slavers in 1862, and the island has belonged to Chile since 1888. In 1990 the population totaled 2130, of whom 1500 were children. Some 69% of the present population is descended from the Maoris, a Polynesian civilization from New Zealand who were among the fiercest opponents of European colonizers.

Unfortunately, and despite the diligence of archeologists, the limited historical data available has so far brought few answers to the fascinating questions raised by the statues of Easter Island.

A group of moais

The headpieces of red volcanic stone come from the Puna Pau volcano, whereas the stone of the statues is from the main volcano of Rano-Raraka.

Morocco

Introductions to Morocco often begin with its imperial cities, whose famed artistic treasures are striking testimony to the passing of successive dynasties. Here, just for a change, we've decided to look at the country's natural assets.

Morocco's history did not begin with those dynasties. Its coastline, on the Mediterranean and the Atlantic, had attracted colonizers since antiquity: already home to the ancestors of today's Berbers, it was first visited by the Phoenicians, who set up centers where they traded with the inland peoples – even though Carthage actually controlled the region at the time. Soon, however, the Carthaginians extended their influence to the kingdom of Mauritania, home of various Berber tribes. Then it was Rome's turn and Tingis – today's Tangier – even became a Roman city. The most impressive legacy of that period is Volubilis, which traded extensively with the mother country: this was a rich province that supplied Rome in particular with farm produce, but with the coming of the Vandals the Romans were driven out. Morocco also became home to large numbers of Jewish refugees fleeing persecution at the hands of Christians. The last wave of invaders was that of the Arabs in the 7th century: for them the Atlantic was to be their ultimate western frontier. The native Berbers often rose in bloody revolt against the Arabs and power tended to alternate between the two camps, the Arabs being weakened by internal conflicts.

Over the next thousand years dynasty succeeded dynasty, all of them – including the Berbers, who had converted to Islam – proclaiming their faith in Allah. The leaders of the principal dynasties were the Idrissids, Fatimids, Almoravids, Merinids and not least the Saadian Princes, who left splendid tombs in Marrakech: such was the wealth they brought to Morocco that their reign can be compared to the Renaissance in Europe. In the 17th century, however, they were driven out by the austere Alawis under Moulay Ismail "the Bloodthirsty", who established the capital at Meknes. With the 19th century came colonization and the awakening of the old tribes, their chiefs and their internal dissensions. Morocco became independent on 2 March 1956.

The Ammeln Valley

200 kilometers (125 miles) from Agadir, the area around the village of Tafraut is a delight to the eye – especially in February, when the almond trees are in blossom. 1200 meters (4000 ft) above sea level, Tafraut is at the foot of a chain of extraordinary granite mountains: this is the jumping-off point for the Ammeln Valley, surrounded by the surrealistic Jebel el Kest, 2200 meters (7250 ft) high. The wealth of this region lies in its olive and almond trees.

Tunisia

Historically speaking the Berbers, now a very small minority in Tunisia, are the oldest known inhabitants of North Africa, dating from the second millennium BC. They were called "barbarians" – meaning "foreigners" – by the Greeks and then by the Romans, and the name has lived on in a deformed version. They call themselves Imazighen, "the free men".

In the 12th century BC Phoenicians from Tyre arrived in Tunisia and founded the cities of Utica, Bizerta and Susa. Later the legendary queen Dido, also known as Elissa, founded Kart-Hadasht – Carthage, the "New City" – in 814 BC: this was the origin of a Semitic civilization that lasted a thousand years and gradually left its mark on the Berbers.

Carthage's trading ships brought back silver from Spain, tin from Cornwall and gold from Guinea, but there was conflict with the Greeks in Sicily, then with the Romans. The Carthaginian fleet was sunk, the city was forced to pay tribute and ultimately had to cope with a rising by its mercenaries.

Despite his victories in Italy, Hannibal was unable to take Rome. Called back to Carthage, he was defeated at Zama by the Roman general Scipio Africanus and his ally, the Berber king Massinissa. Defeat did not halt Carthage's trading activities, however, and the Roman politician Cato took to closing his speeches with the famous words Carthago delenda est: "Carthage must be destroyed".

After a siege lasting three years the city finally fell to Scipio Emilianus in 146 BC, and was razed.

Tunisia is home to splendid mosaics dating from Roman times, as well as temples, triumphal arches, forums, theatres and not least amphitheaters, of which El Jem is the most famous.

Dougga, called Thugga in ancient times, was already a large city during the rule of the Numidian king Massinissa.

The Libyan-Carthaginian tomb there is the only one of its kind: dating from the 3rd century BC, it is 21 meters (70 ft) high, with Ionic pilasters and sculptures of horsemen on its third story. It is topped with a pyramid with a statue of a winged genie at each corner.

The Roman part of Dougga is one of the best-preserved in all Africa, with monuments dating from the 3rd and 2nd centuries BC. The theater has remained relatively intact, with seating for 3500. Facing the plain,

El Jem

This magnificent amphitheater is a reminder of the major economic role – farm produce, olives – of a province the Romans covered with civil and religious monuments. The El Jem amphitheater is almost as big as the Coliseum and larger than the Roman arena in Nîmes, France. Under the Romans El Jem was known as Thysdrus.

the Capitol has a handsome, six-column portico and a shrine dedicated to the Jupiter-Juno-Minerva trinity.

On Windrose Square you can see the name of the twelve winds cut into the stone. The temple of Juno Caelestis was previously home to the mysteries of the Carthaginian goddess Tanit. The arches of Septimus Severus and Severus Alexander still stand, in memory of these Roman emperors of Berber extraction.

Egypt: Gizeh

The Pyramids and the Sphinx

After trying different sorts of pyramid – stepped at Saqqarah, tower-shaped at Meidum, a rhomboid at Dahshur – the Egyptians found perfection at Gizeh. The Pyramid of Cheops is the only one of the Seven Wonders of the World to have survived.

A few miles south of Cairo, on the Gizeh plateau, the pharaohs of the 4th dynasty found the site for their burial monument. Here on the edge of the Libyan Desert stand the three great pyramids, homes to the secrets of kings who died almost 4500 years ago.

The idea of being buried in a pyramid goes back to the time of Jeser (or Zoser), first pharaoh of the 3rd dynasty and his personal architect Imhotep, inventor of the Egyptian use of stone. During the Early Empire the

Egyptians made their sun-god and creator Ra the first of their divinities. When the sovereign died, they believed, he would rejoin his solar father.

As the supreme representation of the ray of sunlight, the pyramid would help the pharaoh approach Ra, then board the sacred boat that would take him through the daily and nightly journeys of the sun.

The pharaoh Snefru, founder of the 4th dynasty built three pyramids at Meidum and Dahshur. The

architectural lessons learnt there quickly led to the plans for the perfect pyramid, of truly colossal dimensions. However it was Snefru's son and successor, Cheops (Khufu), who ultimately built this extraordinary monument.

The pyramid of Cheops so impressed travelers that it found a place among the Wonders of the Ancient World. The statistics are striking: 230 meters (760 ft) square at the base; 137 meters (450 ft) at its peak; and no fewer than 2,300,000 separate blocks of stone, each averaging two and a half tonnes. Such is the achievement of Akhet Khufu – "Cheops is luminous" – as the Egyptians called the Great Pyramid.

Not far away are the pyramids of Cheops' successors Khafre-Ur ("Khafre the Great") and Menkaure-Netjer ("Menkaure the God"). While smaller, they remain extremely imposing.

The rest of the plateau is crisscrossed with alleyways of mastabas, tombs of high officials. Decorated with scenes of everyday life, the chapels of these tombs are sources of priceless information on how people lived in Egypt in those distant times.

Beside the Khafre Valley temple the Sphinx, guardian of the burial ground, surveys the puny humans who, for 4500 years, have been visiting the eternal pharaohs.

Tutankhamen

No name is more evocative of grandeur, wealth and magnificence than that of Tutankhamen. And yet no one could have guessed that this young pharaoh was destined for such fame: his role in Egyptian history was a minor one and his reign extremely brief.

Tutankhamen appears to have been a cousin or nephew of Akhenaton (crowned under the name Amenophis IV), the mystical pharaoh who set out to make the sun-god Aton the ruling divinity of the dynasty and so rein in the power of the clergy of Amon.

Not long before his death, Akhenaton named the husband of his daughter Smenkhare co-regent.

However, the husband seems not to have outlived his father-in-law, which left the young Tutankhamen the sole pretender to the throne. To strengthen his power base, Tutankhamen married Akhenaton's second daughter Ankhesenpaaton.

At this time he was only sixteen and under the influence of an entourage extremely hostile to the sun-god heresy that had been preached by Akhenaton.

As a result he abandoned Aton and devoted himself to the worship of Amon. However he was a sickly youth and died two years later after suffering concussion.

As custom required, he was buried in the Valley of the Kings, in a chamber originally intended for his direct successor Ay, holder of the hereditary title of Divine Father.

Hidden behind the rubble left by the excavation of the tomb of Ramses VI, Tutankhamen's grave remained totally forgotten until 1922, when it was discovered by Howard Carter and Lord Carnarvon.

For five years the two Englishmen had suspected the existence of the tomb, having found engraved amulets bearing the name of Tutankhamen near the tombs of Ramses VI and Ramses IX.

It was when they came upon a step cut into the rock, on 4 September 1922, that their theory was justified.

Compared to the vast tombs of the Ramses – some of them were 100 meters (330 ft) long, that of Tutankhamen is very small indeed.

The staircase led to a long, sloping corridor leading in turn to a vestibule; this was followed by a storeroom, the burial chamber itself and yet another small room. Such was the site of Carter's treasure.

It is hard to imagine, when you see the treasure on display in the Cairo Museum, how it could all have fitted into four rooms. In addition, the archeologists' reports seemed to indicate that no attempt had been made to arrange the objects, which were simply heaped up on top of each other.

It is now known, in fact, that in the early 20th Dynasty, the tomb had been raided by robbers, who had been almost caught in the act and had fled, leaving their hastily piled up booty behind.

An inventory was made and the tomb was then sealed; the seals were discovered intact by the Egyptologists who opened it again.

So it can be said fairly accurately that we possess all the objects placed there when the young Tutankhamen was buried.

When the tomb was opened the burial chamber was the main source of admiration and wonderment. True, the existence of such beautiful objects was already known, but in terms of sheer quantity the tomb of Tutankhamen went far beyond anybody's wildest imaginings.

Four wooden chapels coated with gold, inlaid with glass paste and fitted one inside the other covered a stone sarcophagus. Underneath, the mummy, wearing a burial mask, lay inside a sequence of three coffins. Made of gilded wood, the two outermost coffins showed the pharaoh in the Osiris pose, with his flail and scepter on his chest.

The inner one was of solid gold, decorated with enamel and precious stones: in all, an object 1.85 meters (6 ft) long that weighed 110 kilograms (250 pounds).

The other rooms were packed with all sorts of pieces made of alabaster, gold, gilt wood, precious and semiprecious stones, ebony and silver: amulets, funeral boats, vases, beds, seats, jewelry, chests and personal finery – all intended to accompany the young Tutankhamen on his journey into the next world.

The burial mask

Traditionally the pharaoh's burial mask included a headdress on which gold alternated with bands of vivid blue lapis lazuli. In the case of Tutankhamen, however – shown here with the face of the god Osiris – only gold has been used, apparently to emphasize his divinity.

Ethiopia

This was the land of the Queen of Sheba. According to the legend, she went to visit Solomon in Jerusalem when he was building the temple there; the king was so taken aback by the magnificence of her caravans – her enormous wealth came from trading in incense – that in spite of his beauty he struck her as a thorough country bumpkin. And this is why she preferred to give birth to his child in her homeland…

Their son, Menelik, would later visit Solomon and ask to be recognized as his son and heir; and during his stay the strange young man stole the Tables of the Law, in order that his mother's country might have the same divine character as his father's.

The name Ethiopia comes from a Greek word meaning "people with burnt faces". At the time it was much larger than today, its northern part including Kush, the land of the Hebrew prophets, and the Greek territory of Meroe. Gradually the Egyptians expanded southwards into the "land of Punt", building a city at Napata and covering the area with monuments in the Egyptian style. This was the period of the "black pharaohs", who made Napata their capital around 930 BC. Later the Persian ruler Cambyses sent his armies into the region and Greek merchants worked the coast of the Red Sea; but the real ordeal came from incursions by the Romans, who burnt Napata in 24-23 BC and established a new capital at Meroe. In the 3rd century AD Ethiopia was occupied by the Nubians and the Blemmyes. This was the era of the splendid kingdom of Axum, which lasted more than a thousand years. Ethiopia became Christian in the 4th century and in the 10th century, after a long period of conflict, a revolution led by a woman, Judith, drove the reigning princes out into the kingdom of Choa. Judith was succeeded by eleven monarchs, one of whom, Lalibela, became famous as a builder of monuments. Then came the return of the refugees from Choa, in spite of an alliance with the Muslims and the Falasha Jews. Prosperity returned to Ethiopia in the 15th century. A century later Islam, with the backing of the Ottoman Empire, began launching attacks on this Christian enclave. It was also at this time that the Portuguese, in search of a route to India, began to take an interest in this mythical country.

Gondar

At the western edge: Ziguinchor, the Casamance border city between Senegal and Guinea-Bissau. At the eastern edge: Djibouti, in Africa, facing Aden, in Asia, on the other side of the Red Sea. On the same latitude, from west to east: Bamako in Mali, Ouagadougou in Burkina Faso, Kano in Nigeria, N'Djamena in Chad, Sannar in Sudan and Gondar in Ethiopia. Less than 2,000km (1250 miles) from the equator: to the west is virgin forest, to the east lies the desert – luxuriant vegetation on the one hand, and bare ground on the other. By Lake Tana stands Gondar, once a palatial city and the capital of Ethiopia. Here we see the ruins of the palace of Fasilidas, first of the Gondar emperors, who ruled from 1632 to 1667. The building style harks back to Ethiopia's Portuguese period: as Christians the Ethiopians were under threat on all sides from Islam and news of their unfailing, irrational resistance reached the Portuguese, then seeking a route to India. The latter had already tried to make contact with the "land of Prester John". The first alliance was signed in 1515, with the Portuguese undertaking to protect the Ethiopians against the Muslims. Nonetheless, Axum was destroyed and the capital was moved to Gondar. At one point Gondar was Africa's second largest city, with a population of 100,000.

Angola

Angola is situated in southwestern Central Africa with, for neighbors, Congo and Zaire to the north, Zambia and Zaire to the east and Namibia to the south. It has 1650 kilometers (1030 miles) of coastline on the Atlantic. In the 10th century AD it was settled by Bantu peoples from what are now Nigeria and Cameroon. The Kongo kingdom, as it was then called, extended over Zaire, Angola, Congo and Gabon. Its capital was Mbanza Kongo, a city in what is now the Zaire province of Angola.

With an area of 1,246,000 square kilometers (500,000 square miles), this is a country offering real climatic variety. The main rivers have their sources on the central Bié plateau, with the Kwanza running into the Atlantic and the Kasai flowing north into Zaire: the Mai Munene Falls are especially beautiful. Other rivers large and small flow in all directions – and there are other waterfalls too: in Malanje province are the striking Kalandula Falls.

In the province of Benguela the Moro Moco mountains climb to 2620 meters (8650 ft). The north of the country – Cabinda province, to be precise – is ruled by dense forest, with more open forest on the plateaux of the interior. Grassy plains are common, although in the south they give way to the poorer grassland of the steppe, and then to the dunes of the Namibian Desert.

The country's flora is extremely varied. In Bengo province you find baobabs, there are cacti on the shoreline in Benguela, and in the Namibian Desert is the extremely rare plant welvitschia mirabilis, described as a "living fossil".

The fauna is just as varied and very numerous. The different provinces now have their own national parks to ensure protection for the different species. The Iona nature reserve, for example, is home to magnificent zebras, while elephants find refuge in the Quissama park in Bengo province. One of the most famous animal attractions is the giant black antelope, a feature of the Kagandula nature reserve.

For those who like going out for a stroll, the little river port of Noki, on the border with Zaire, is only one of many interesting spots. And of course the river Zaire itself is a spectacle no visitor should miss.

Kalandula Falls

The cascade at Kalandula might be smaller than Victoria Falls, but it is very impressive all the same. Situated in Malanje province, in northwestern Angola, this was called in colonial times the "Duke of Bragança" Falls, as a tribute to the Portuguese royal family.

The Seychelles

Jean Moreau de Sécheles, Louis XV's Supervisor of Finances, would be more than surprised to see this archipelago – 92 volcanic islands and coral atolls, lost in the Indian Ocean northeast of Madagascar – with its present status as a tourist paradise. Arab merchants set up here and in the 16th and 17th centuries the Seychelles were a port of call on the way to India. They also served as a refuge for pirates.

The archipelago was only properly explored in the 18th century on instructions from Mahé de la Bourdonnais, governor general of the Mascareigne Islands. The largest of the Seychelles bears his name and two others, Praslin and Silhouette were also named in honor of officers of the King.

Mahé and Praslin, the two main islands, are surrounded by a sprinkling of others, including the spectacular Bird Island, a tiny refuge, 2 square kilometers (1 square mile), for numerous seabirds, and Cousin and Cousine islands, both magnificent nature reserves and home to different kinds of terns, seagulls, frigate birds, hummingbirds and many others.

Made of pink granite, Praslin is 36 kilometers (23 miles) from Mahé. Here we find the famous May Valley, a superb nature park full of orchids, giant flowers and a host of trees: acacias and all sorts of palms, including latanias and the unique "coco de mer". Another marvelous place is Aldabra, the largest coral atoll in the world, with a lagoon 30 kilometers (19 miles) long. Here you find giant turtles that can live to be 200 years old and weigh up to 300 kilograms (670 pounds).

This is indeed a land of white sandy beaches, crystal lagoons, coral reefs, fish of all colors, rocks of the strangest shapes, coconut palms, and exotic flowers and wildlife; and when the tourist brochures wax ecstatic about the Seychelles – even if the clichés are still clichés – they are only telling the truth about the natural assets of a group of islands Nature has showered with gifts.

Unsurprisingly, luxury tourism has now become part of the economy of the Seychelles, where the local industries – fishing, tea planting, cultivation of vanilla and cinnamon – were often not enough to meet people's needs.

Mahé

The islands of the Indian Ocean have thousands upon thousands of miles of coastline with clear water, fine sandy beaches, forests of palms and the shelter of coconut trees. This natural paradise lies northeast of Madagascar.

Australia

Often compared to a gigantic raft sitting astride the Tropic of Capricorn, Australia is the largest island in the world: from north to south it measures 3200 kilometers (2000 miles) and from east to west 3850 kilometers (2400 miles).

In the heart of the continent, some 450 km (280 miles) southwest of Alice Springs, lies our planet's biggest monolith: Ayers Rock or Uluru, as the Aboriginal people – once again its proprietors, after 200 years of white "ownership" – call it. Believed to be 600 million years old, this gigantic mass of sandstone is 348 meters (1150 ft) high, with a perimeter of 9 km (6 miles).

It is now a major tourist attraction; not surprisingly, given the spectacular displays of color it offers, shifting from yellow to purple in the course of the day. According to the Aboriginal legend, the color is due to the blood spilt during a battle between giant snakes.

Hunter-gatherers whose life had deep roots in myth and ritual, Australia's Aboriginal people probably arrived from South-East Asia at least 40,000 years ago. Uluru remains for them a sacred site: only initiated men are allowed access to the rock and its many caves, decorated with paintings portraying the everyday existence of the local tribes. The grueling initiation rites are based on the notions of death and rebirth.

Religious ceremonies are in the hands of the Elders, who have a profound knowledge of their tribe's "Dreaming", a creation myth in which the sun, the moon and everyday animals – the wallaby, the snake, the dingo, the kangaroo – play a fundamental part. The omnipresent Rainbow Serpent is the symbol of fertility, while the Sky Heroes are mankind's first totemic ancestors. Each clan bears the name of its totem, which helps and protects clan members.

Rituals often take the form of mimes and dances during which the participants communicate with the spirits of the dead.

Never very numerous, the Aboriginal community now numbers some 150,000. A few still live the life of their ancestors, others live on reserves. Those deprived of their tribal territory often find themselves living under extremely difficult urban conditions.

Ayers Rock

Ayers Rock is one of the world's most spectacular sites. Now part of the Uluru National Park, it is set in the heart of Australia's "Red Center". It has been a sacred mountain for the Aboriginal people for at least 40,000 years – Europeans only came to Australia in the late 18th century.

The Seven Wonders of the World

It is hardly surprising that the first list of the Wonders of the World was made up of sites and monuments spread around the Mediterranean basin: it was drawn up by a Greek author. Of the seven, however, only the Pyramid of Gizeh – chronologically the oldest – has survived. The Egyptians began building pyramids as burial sites for their pharaohs and queens in 2780 BC, during the rule of Jeser, or Zoser as he was also called. Styles and techniques developed over the next 1200 years, culminating in the Pyramid of Gizeh, built near Cairo for the pharaoh Cheops: 146 meters (480 ft) high and comprising no less than 2,500,000 blocks of stone weighing between two and three tonnes each.

By comparison the Hanging Gardens of Babylon were a recent venture, built in the 6th century BC on the fertile plains of Mesopotamia, or modern Iraq. Set on the banks of the Euphrates, Babylon had had its heyday as a cultural and trading capital a thousand years earlier; but after a long period of conflict and decline, it temporarily regained something of its old splendor under Nabopolassar, whose son Nebuchadnezzar was a great builder. The famous "hanging" gardens spoken of in Herodotus' history were in fact the ornate terraces of step-built palaces. Elaborate irrigation systems allowed for the cultivation of luxuriant vegetation and exotic, highly perfumed plants.

According to legend, Alexander the Great was born the day a madman set fire to the Temple of Artemis at Ephesus, in 356 BC. Built two centuries earlier in what is now Turkey, this temple was dedicated to the hunter-goddess known to the Romans as Diana. Artemis/Diana was also a symbol of fertility. Absolutely enormous – 110 meters (360 ft) long and 50 meters (165 ft) wide – it was surrounded by a double row of columns 20 meters (66 ft) high and richly ornamented. It was a famous place of pilgrimage and Alexander, originally from Macedonia where Artemis was widely worshipped, had the once-sumptuous building restored when he and his armies entered Asia Minor in 334 BC.

Alexander's trail of conquests continued on to Halicarnassus, a little further to the south. Here, in the home country of Herodotus, a governor named Mausolus had begun building a giant tomb for himself; however, at his death in 353 BC the tomb was still unfinished and the work was continued by his queen Artemisia – who was also, in accordance with the custom of the time, his sister. Ultimately the two lay side by side in the white marble building topped by a chariot and horses 40 meters (130 ft) above the ground. Mausolus' burial complex was so striking that the Mausoleum at Halicarnassus, one of the Seven Wonders of the World, gave us the word still used today for such buildings.

Apart from being the city of the games, held there every four years from the 7th century BC, Olympia was the religious capital of Ancient Greece. It was there, in the 5th century BC, that Phidias, sculptor and architect, created a statue of Zeus – the chief of all the Gods – of unequalled size and beauty. Phidias was clearly the man for the job, having been mainly responsible for the building of Pericles' Athens: at the height of his glory the great strategist wanted a dazzling home for Socrates, Sophocles, Herodotus and Anaxagoras. The Statue of Zeus at Olympia has long since disappeared, but the friezes of the Parthenon live on as testimony to Phidias' extraordinary talent. It was towards the end of his life that he sculpted the 12-meter (40 ft) ivory figure of the god of gods, seating it on a wooden throne inlaid with gold and precious stones. Zeus' hair and beard were of gold and the statue drew enormous crowds of visitors.

Chares, creator of the Colossus of Rhodes in approximately 300 BC, never found the same fame as Phidias, even though his 35-meter (115 ft) statue of Helios – the sun god and protector of the island of Rhodes – dominated the port of Lindos. At the time Rhodes was a sea power with trading posts everywhere, and it may be that the statue was erected to celebrate the Rhodians' resistance to the Greek fleet. Created at ground level, the various parts of the structure were then raised and assembled one by one, right up to the crowned head that makes you think of the Statue of Liberty in New York. Sixty years after its completion the Colossus was brought low by an earthquake, most of it doubtless falling into the sea. Several expeditions have been organized to search for the remains, but without success.

Another name that evokes all the power, splendor and intellectual prowess of the past is that of Alexandria. Established in the Nile delta by Alexander the Great, the city, with its straight streets and imposing temples and buildings, was intended as a pure symbol of its founder's might. It was there that Ptolemy I, Alexander's successor, created a museum and the famous library of 700,000 parchment scrolls.

The greatest wonder of Alexandria, however, was its lighthouse. Ptolemy II linked the island of Pharos to the mainland by a causeway – a project Alexander had once considered – and by approximately 280 BC had finished the construction, on the causeway, of a spectacular tower: three stories of white marble – 100 meters (330 ft) in all – whose apex was a circular peristyle where two fires burned all night every night. All who saw it were stunned by its sheer scale – but like most of the Seven Wonders, it was doomed to destruction in an earthquake.

Another famous Ptolemy of Alexandria was the astronomer, mathematician and geographer who lived there in approximately 87-150 AD. He had already grasped the principle of the rotation of the earth and his work found expression in two books vital to early studies of our planet and the universe: Mathematical Syntaxis (widely called the Almagest), a thirteen-book mathematical treatment of the phenomena of astronomy, and Geography, which remained the principal work on the subject until the time of Columbus.

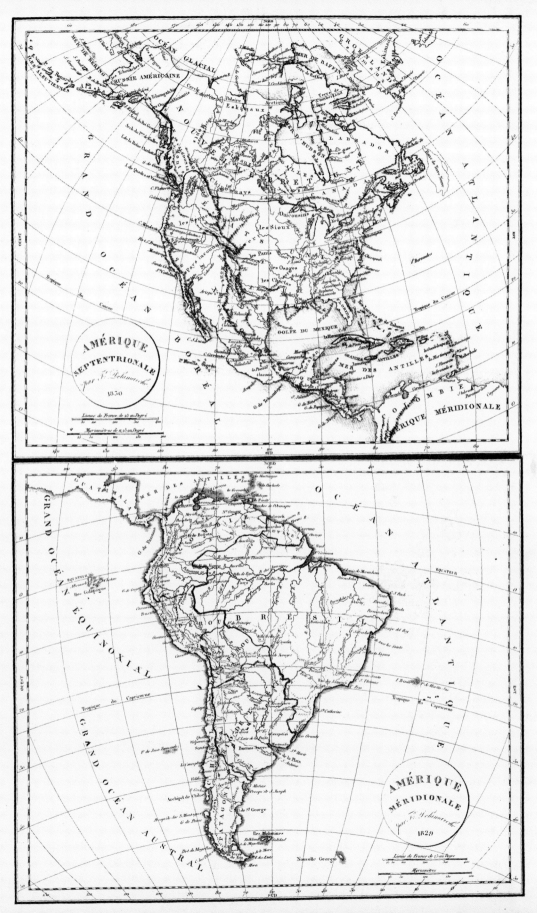

115

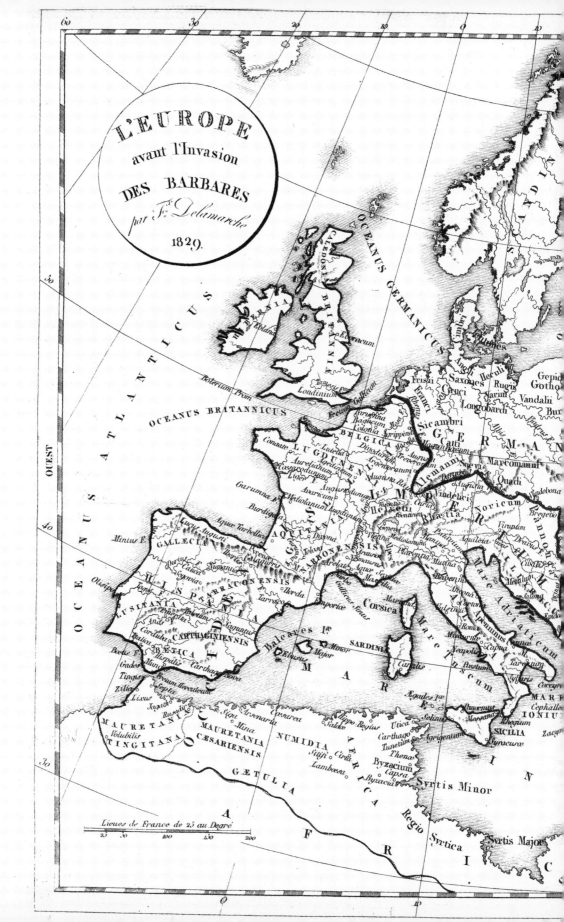

L'EUROPE
avant l'Invasion
DES BARBARES
par F.ᵉ Delamarche
1829.

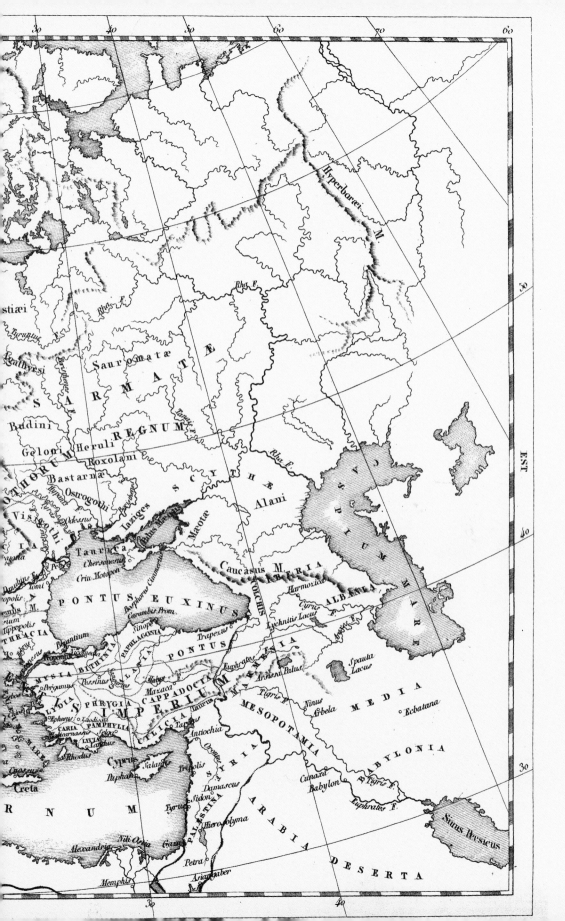

stiæi

Turuntus

Agathyrsi

Badini

Geloni Heruli REGNUM

Borysthenes

OTHORUM

Bastarnæ

Ostrogothi

Hypanis

Bazdagus

VIS Ardus

Visigothi

Odessus

Tomi

Danubius M.

Tomi

THRACIA

Byzantium

Propontis

Nicomedia

Cyzicus

MYSIA BITHYNIA

Pergamus

LYDIA

Ephesus

Laodicea

CARIA PHRYGIA

Halicarnassus

Gnidus

LYCIA

Rhodus

Creta

RNUM

Salamis

Paphos

Cyprus

Alexandria

Nili Ostia Gaza

Memphis

Ariasgaber

SARMATÆ

Sauromatæ

Peuceynes

Tanarus F.

SCYTHÆ

Maeotæ

Alani

Tauria

Iaziges

Chersonesus Cimmerius

Sinus Maeotis

Criu Metopon

PONTUS EUXINUS

Bosphorus Cimmerius

Carambis Prom.

Sinope

Trapezus

CAPPADOCIA

Maxaca

Halys F.

Pessinus

Tapsus

CILICIA Taurus

Antiochia

Orontes

SYRIA

PALÆSTINA

Hiero olyma

Tripolis

Damascus

Sidon

Tyrus

Petra

Rha F.

Rha F.

Rha F.

COLCHIS

Caucasus M.

IBERIA

Harmozica

ALBANIA

Cyrus F.

Lychnitis Lacus

Araxes F.

ARMENIA

Euphrates F.

Tigris F.

Ninus

Arbela

MESOPOTAMIA

Cunaxa

Babylon

Euphrates F.

Tigris F.

Hyperborei M.

CASPIUM MARE

Spauta Lacus

Arissa Palus

MEDIA

Ecbatana

BABYLONIA

ARABIA

DESERTA

Sinus Persicus

EST

117

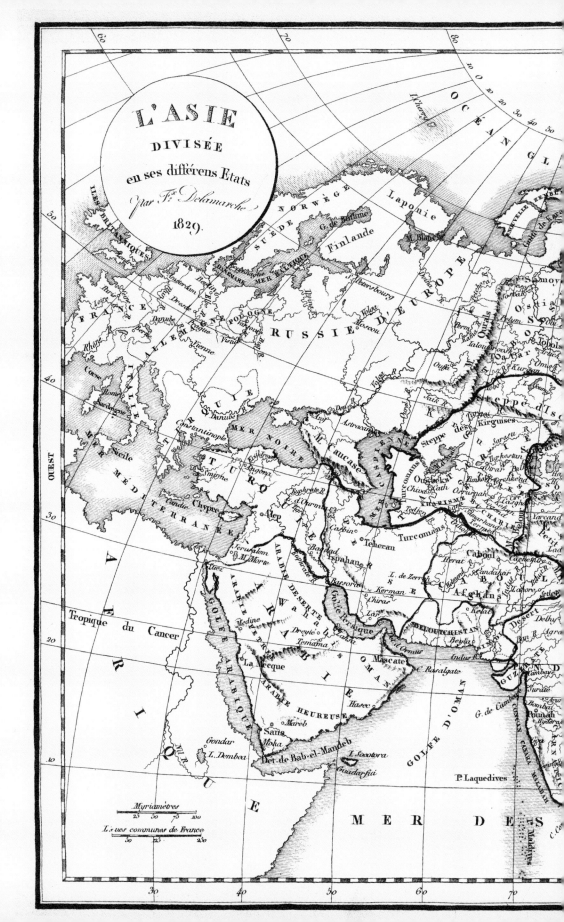

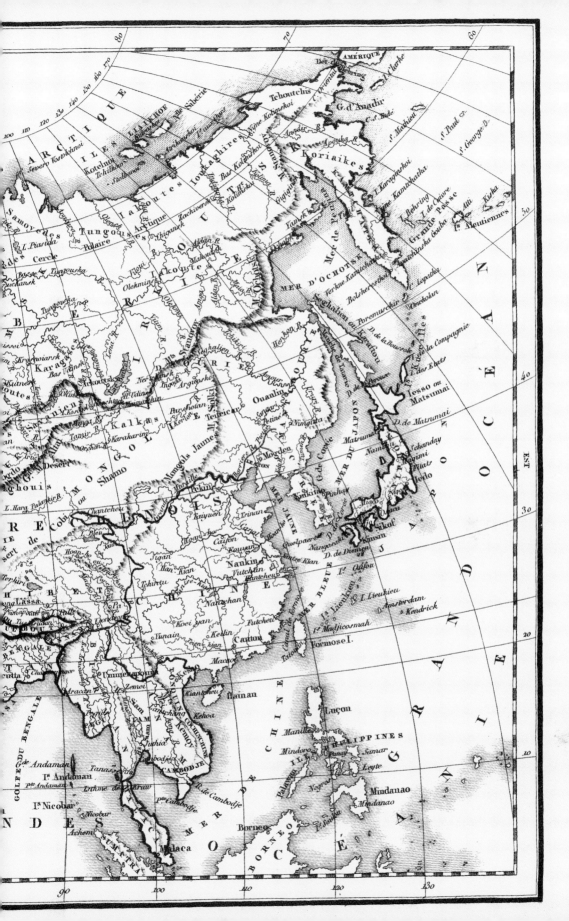

119

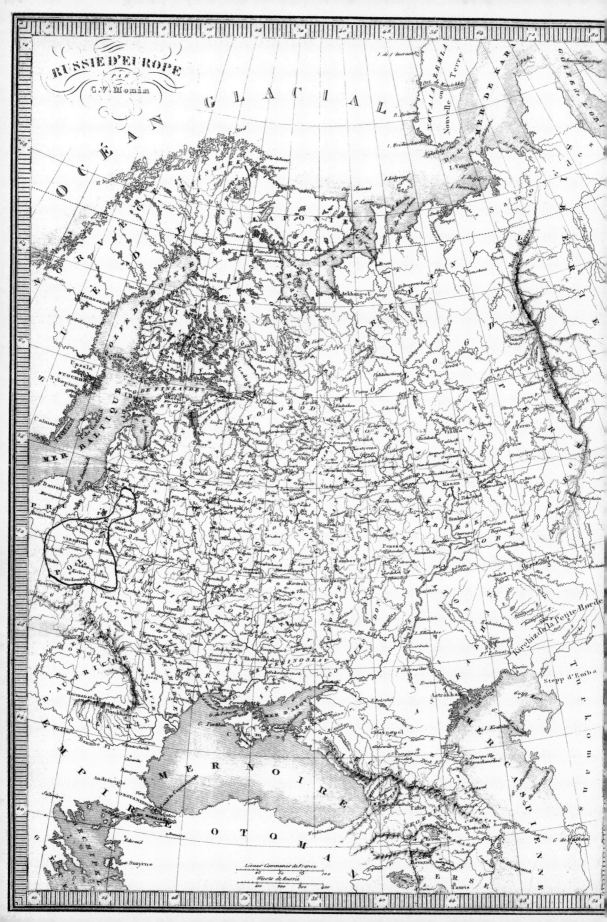

IMAGINARY MODEL

OF ANCIENT JERUSALEM